THE VILLAGE SHOP

THE VILLAGE SHOP

Jonathan Brown
Sadie Ward

RURAL DEVELOPMENT COMMISSION
in association with
CAMERON & HOLLIS
and
DAVID & CHARLES

Published on behalf of the Rural Development Commission,
141 Castle Street, Salisbury, Wiltshire SP1 3TP
by Cameron & Hollis, PO Box 1, Moffat, Dumfriesshire DG10 9SU,
the publishing imprint of Cameron Books,
in association with David & Charles plc, Brunel House, Newton Abbot,
Devon TQ12 4PU.
Distributed by David & Charles

Edited by Jill Hollis
Designed by Ian Cameron

Colour reproduction by Brian Gregory Associates, St Albans
Monochrome reproduction by BB Associates, Chichester
Printed and bound by MacLehose & Partners Ltd, Portsmouth

ISBN 0-906506-03-4

Printed in England

Frontispiece: Milton Abbas Post Office during the judging for the Dorset Best Kept Village Competition, 1989.

Jacket pictures. Front: Village shop and post office, Stanton Harcourt, Oxfordshire, 1989. *Back:* Nestlé Smokers Chocoloate Bar, 1930s.

PREFACE

There have been village shops of one sort or another for something like 400 years. Discovering their past is not a straightforward task: records are few, and detailed research has barely begun. What follows, therefore, does not claim to be a detailed history, rather a series of portraits at different stages in the village shop's development. We concentrate on the general retailer, the seller of groceries, drapery and hardware, who was usually the principal shopkeeper of the village. Others engaged in more specialist retail trades – the butcher, the baker, chemist and greengrocer – make their appearance, but those such as the tailor and publican, whose retailing activities were peripheral to craft or service trades, have not been covered. A theme central to this account is the way in which village shopkeeping has adapted to the changing circumstances of country life, often in the face of some difficulty. If this book stimulates interest in, and further research into the contribution of the shopkeeper to the life of rural England, it will have served its purpose.

Contents

1994 Addendum

Readers are reminded that this book was originally published in 1990.
Much of the information on both statutory requirements and assistance available
from organisations such as the Rural Development Commission has changed.

Butter at its very best

I**T'S SPRING TIME** in New Zealand and, already, the first consignments of new season's butter have arrived in this country. This delicious butter is literally a store-house of *natural* health-giving vitamins, for it is made under ideal conditions of warm sunshine and fresh green pasturelands. During the sunless months ahead give your family plenty of New Zealand butter . . . so aptly described as "solid sunshine."

Ask for it by name

NEW ZEALAND BUTTER

Foreword

Until a few years ago the presence of shops in our villages could be taken for granted. During the 1970s and 1980s, however, much has changed. The growth of car ownership among more fortunate village residents and the development of supermarkets in or near the main towns has led to a sharp decline in the numbers of independent retailers. Dr Ward points out that 'probably a quarter of rural communities no longer have the benefit of a convenient village shop'; and recent research for the Rural Development Commission shows that the proportion is even higher in several of the more remote rural counties. There appears to have been some slow-down in the rate of loss in the past few years, but only as a result of the opening of new-style shops selling such things as crafts and home-made foods, often mainly for the benefit of visitors.

With the future of traditional village shops very much 'on the line', the appearance of this scholarly but readable history is most timely. Its account of the rise of village shops together with an investigation of the difficulties that afflict their owners today contribute to an important, fascinating and little researched part of English social history. The efforts of the Rural Development Commission, Rural Community Councils and local authorities to help to arrest their decline are well worth setting down.

Mainly, though, I welcome this opportunity to bring the story to a wider audience. Local facilities, like pubs, shops and post offices, are what make the difference between a community and a dormitory. Those readers who live in or visit the countryside can help to ensure the survival of real village communities by using local facilities. What we hand on to the next generation is the responsibility of us all.

It is with great pleasure that I acknowledge the financial assistance of Anchor Foods and Smiths Food Group. Without their help and co-operation, a much less attractive book would have appeared.

Lord Vinson of Roddam Dene

Origins

Before the arrival of shops in the countryside retailing was largely carried out by itinerant tradesmen who drove carts or rode ponies or simply walked from market to market, and from village to village. As communications were slow and difficult, obtaining a regular supply of goods from any distance was on the whole not practicable, and there was a high degree of local self-sufficiency as far as basic needs were concerned. Throughout the medieval period and up until the eighteenth century it was the travellers who provided the best, indeed almost the only, means of satisfying household needs in the countryside. These were the people known as chapmen, although by the eighteenth century the term was declining in favour of pedlar, hawker, cheapjack or tallyman.

There were also chapwomen. A modest number of wills of such people survive from the seventeenth and early eighteenth centuries. One was left by Elizabeth Lawrence of Donington-on-Bain in Lincolnshire whose stock-in-trade when she died in 1670 consisted of a small supply of pins, needles, buttons, cotton, tape, laces and combs. A number of these pedlar women spent a working lifetime going the rounds of the villages. Dorothy Wordsworth, sister of the famous poet, recorded in her journal in 1800 that 'the Cockermouth traveller came with thread, hardware, mustard, etc. She is very healthy; has travelled over the mountains these thirty years'. This woman always walked. She had apparently wanted an ass, but her husband regarded such an animal as demeaning and not worthy of her status as a responsible trader.

Chapmen could become reasonably well off. When James Pilkington of Barrow-on-Humber died in 1635, his estate was worth the substantial sum of £242. He had become a farmer and owned 21 acres of land and some cattle. The exact nature of the business that had brought him such wealth cannot be told, for the assessors of the probate simply recorded 'wares', but he had traded, with his horse and pack saddle, in villages as far as forty or fifty miles from home.

For many, perhaps most itinerants, business was conducted principally by touring around various markets. For all but the most remote of the population there was a market town within comfortable day-tripping distance, which for those who travelled on foot meant ten miles away at most. Retail markets were held once a week (or twice or even three times a week in the larger towns), and country folk came to them to do much of their regular shopping.

By the nineteenth century, the better-class chapmen – of James Pilkington's substance – had come to be known as cheapjacks. Often based in a large town, the cheapjack rode out with his horse and cart laden with the products of, for example, Sheffield and Birmingham industry. One man, who published his memoirs in 1876, recalled setting out with at least £100 worth of penknives, cutlery, padlocks, bridles, whips and the like. He also recorded having travelled considerable distances. Starting from London, this man would reach Norwich for its Saturday market ten days later, calling on the way at markets in Romford,

Early 19th-century pedlar doll.

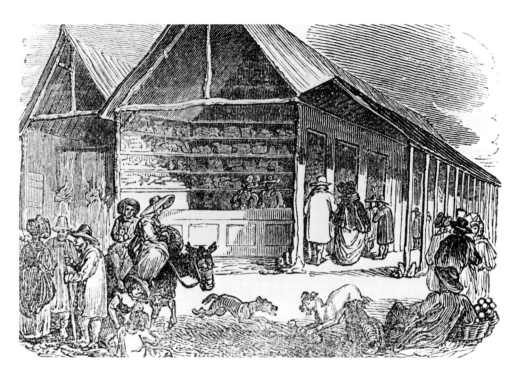

Sturbridge Fair depicted in a Book of Days published in the 1830s.

Bishops Stortford, Chelmsford, Colchester, Hadleigh, Bury St Edmunds and Diss. Later, he bought a bigger cart with a stronger horse and travelled even further afield.

But the majority of the travelling traders at markets were petty hawkers and pedlars who were lucky if they had a pack pony, and were more likely to carry on their backs the job lots of cheap crockery, ornaments and jewellery which they acquired from city warehouses and 'swag' shops. Once at a market, they would set out their wares and holler out an elaborate patter of far-fetched stories involving shipwrecks, fires and the like from which the goods now on offer had been rescued at no small cost to the body and pocket of the salesman. Crowds gathered, mostly for the free entertainment, but enough were persuaded to buy to keep the hawkers in business.

There were fairs, too, which the hawkers, pedlars and chapmen regularly attended. Most market towns had at least one fair a year at which general domestic goods, hardware and toys were traded. Usually they took place in autumn or spring, times when people would be stocking up in advance of, or following, the disruption of supplies caused by winter weather. In the larger towns, these fairs could be enormous gatherings, combining retail and wholesale trade, with manufacturers, merchants and shopkeepers meeting at them to clinch deals. By far the largest of these was Sturbridge, which was held in a field just outside Cambridge and lasted for three weeks during August and September. The retail stalls were arranged as a street called Cheapside, noted by the author Daniel Defoe as extending for nearly half a mile when he visited the fair in 1722: 'Scarce any trades are omitted', he declared, 'goldsmiths, toyshops, brasiers, turners, milliners, haberdashers, hatters, mercers, drapers, pewtrers, china-warehouses, and in a word all trades that can be named in London'. Beyond these stalls were further rows where the wholesale clothiers, woollen merchants and others had their tents.

Great fairs such as Sturbridge were of limited use to the common people of the villages, but heavily patronised by the gentry and corporate bodies such as the Oxford and Cambridge colleges who bought bulk supplies of groceries and domestic hardware for their large households. There were, however, dozens of smaller, more intimate fairs at which the local people could purchase their household goods.

About fifty fairs for 'petty chapmen' and pedlary were listed for Norfolk alone in the 1830s. Some of these were in the major towns but many were in smaller places. Walsingham, which had once enjoyed urban status but was now a large village of a thousand inhabitants, had one. Horning, with a population of 460, had never been a market town, yet had its little fair on the Monday after 2nd

Burford Fair, Oxfordshire, early 20th century.

A pedlar selling song sheets from village to village.

August. Frettenham held one on the first Monday in April, and at Broomhill, a farm hamlet in the parish of Weeting, there was a fair every 7th July.

By the end of the eighteenth century the pedlary fairs were definitely on the wane. Sturbridge was a shadow of the grand event it had been in Daniel Defoe's day, and many of the village fairs were in decline. Improvements to roads, and the building of canals brought more regular supplies of goods to the country-side. But it was the railway that finally killed off the fairs, bringing the shopkeepers in market towns and villages within easy reach of the wholesalers. Some fairs lingered on, and a handful have survived, although they have now become either cattle fairs or pleasure fairs with few, if any, of the old-fashioned petty chapmen selling cheap trinkets and hardware among the side stalls.

As well as attending fairs, many itinerants travelled round the villages, calling on people at home or setting up a pitch in a convenient central spot to sell pins and needles, matches, small toys and song sheets to the cottagers. Tinkers went round with barrows carrying a grindstone for sharpening knives, and tools for mending pots and pans. Gypsies called to sell clothes pegs and lavender bags. More substantial chapmen and travelling salesmen, reported Daniel Defoe, 'do also keep shops or chambers, or warehouses in the adjacent market towns, and sell their goods in the villages round'. This was the method commonly used for selling fish to villagers. Pack drapers, by now respectable enough to be listed in local trade directories, were also prominent among these traders. In the 1880s, Richard Jefferies wrote that they had 'no shop window, and make no display, but employ several men carrying packs, who work through the villages on foot, and range over a wide stretch of country'. Flora Thompson recalled in *Lark Rise to Candleford* the activities of another local trader who visited Lark Rise selling furniture, and made quite a few sales to the cottage folk because of the generous credit he provided.

By the late nineteenth century, itinerant traders were beginning to disappear as improved communications and frequent, regular supplies of goods made fixed shops a more convenient way of trading for buyer and seller alike, although a few itinerants survive to this day in the shape of the butchers' and fishmongers' vans which go the rounds of some rural areas.

Village shops were first recorded in the late sixteenth century. Probate records show a clear increase in rural England in the number of tradesmen with settled retail businesses. Most were in the market towns, both large and small, but by 1600 a few had become established in the larger villages. Some have been noted in East Anglia – in villages such as South Creake in Norfolk and Botesdale in Suffolk – and some in Gloucestershire. There are also records of haberdashers at Wrightington, Harleton and Burscough and of shoemakers at Eccles, Eskrigg and Ribchester, all in Lancashire. In the course of the seventeenth century, the numbers of such tradesmen gradually increased, and they began to set up businesses in medium-sized and even small villages. By the 1680s, the trend was so well established that a pamphleteer could claim that 'in every country village where is (it may be) not above ten houses, there is a shopkeeper'. There was polemical exaggeration here, for the writer was arguing that village shops were destroying the trade of market towns – a somewhat wild claim but indicative of the fact that village shops were by now fairly commonplace.

The distinctions between manufacture, wholesale trade and retail selling were often blurred in the late 17th century. Butchers, for example, often held land in or near the village on which to pasture the stock they were to slaughter and sell. While the probate inventories refer to the butcher's shop in the village, it is likely that this was a workroom where the meat was jointed and prepared for sale rather than a retail store. Indeed, although some of the butcher's trade would have been in the village, most of his income probably came from business in the market town where he would have had a stall in the market or a booth in what was known as 'the shambles' – a covered building set aside for butchers. In addition there were sales on wholesale terms to drovers and dealers who took the stock away, most often to London.

Shoemakers, basketmakers, carpenters making furniture and a host of other craftsmen who made most of what they sold, would also sell wholesale or retail as appropriate. A few craftsmen developed more varied businesses. The original function of tallow chandlers, for example, was making and selling candles, but seventeenth-century inventories show that chandlers also held stocks of other wares which they evidently had for sale. Groceries such as spices, raisins, honey, vinegar and soap, and ironmongery were among the principal goods listed. Perhaps they had taken on these lines to make up for reduced sales of candles in the summer. In any case, tallow chandlers were clearly becoming general retailers rather than remaining straightforward craftsmen.

There were others whose business was principally retail. Towards the end of the seventeenth century, tradesmen's wills mention drapers (dealers in woollen and linen cloth) and mercers (dealers in silks), as well as ironmongers, and an occasional grocer, a term which referred quite specifically to wholesalers – those who dealt in goods in units of a gross. But a glance at the inventories for these businesses shows that there was an overall tendency towards general retailing. Stephen Alvery of Kirton in Holland (Lincolnshire), who died in 1685, was described as a mercer, but he stocked a wide range of groceries, including such items as figs, prunes, anchovies and candied peel, as well as horseshoes and bellows, tobacco, drugs and medicines, pairs of spectacles with cases, testaments, psalters and primers.

Most of the items listed in shopkeepers' inventories of the seventeenth and eighteenth centuries were luxury goods. Spices, anchovies, silks and psalters, even tea and coffee, were all priced well beyond the means of labourers, whose wages (in many parts of the country no more than 8s or 9s a week in the late eighteenth century) stretched little further than the basics of bread, flour, cheese and essential household goods. It is apparent, then, that the village shop of this time must have been vastly different from what it was later to become. The poor made their purchases at the markets and from the pedlars, and the village shopkeeper drew his custom almost exclusively from the gentry, the wealthy farmers and clergy – people with the income to afford the finer types of grocery, people who could read and therefore might buy the testaments and primers, and even spectacles for when their eyes became strained. In all probability the shop would have been a room in a cottage or an outbuilding where callers could come to buy at those times when the tradesman was not away at the fairs or attending to his wholesale business. This rather exclusive type of village shopkeeping remained until the railway brought the mass market to rural England.

James Moore was a local of Wadebridge, Cornwall. Illustration taken from a postcard published by J.E. Oatley, Wadebridge, c.1920.

The Golden Age: 1800-1880

By the 1820s and 1830s there were few villages from which the retail trades were completely absent. This much is clear from the census returns and trade directories of the time, though an accurate assessment of exactly what line of business particular shops were in is more difficult because of the inconsistency with which people described their own occupations.

The number of shops continued to increase, at least in the larger villages, up to the 1870s. Corby, ten miles to the south east of Grantham in Lincolnshire, was one example. In medieval times there had been a market here, and the village remained a local centre for smaller communities within a radius of three or four miles. In 1826 there were six retailers, by 1850 there were twelve, including five grocers, a baker, a miller and a druggist-cum-wine merchant, while in 1861 there were twenty – a three-fold increase in thirty-five years. A similar trend was evident in villages like Ampleforth and Great Ayton in the North Riding of

H.Quick's bakery and small grocery store in Chipstable, Somerset, in the 1880s.

Yorkshire where the number of shopkeepers more than doubled between 1820 and 1879. Not all villages showed the same rapid increase in retailers, but the indications are that on the whole village shopkeeping was expanding.

More striking than any changes in the total number of shops was the universal increase in the number of general grocery and household stores. Gone were the businesses described as mercers and tallow chandlers. Drapers remained in modest numbers, as did butchers, but they paled beside the growing number of those described as grocers, general dealers and shopkeepers. By the 1870s almost half of the shops in large villages were general retailers. At Thatcham in Berkshire, six out of fourteen retailers were described as shopkeepers or grocers. At Eynsham, a particularly large village in Oxfordshire with a population of 2,000, eleven out of twenty-five were general shopkeepers. In smaller villages with a limited range of trades, the general shopkeeper was even more prominent. Chalgrove in Oxfordshire had two grocers, one general shopkeeper and a baker to serve its 500 inhabitants, while at Woolstone in Berkshire there was only one general shopkeeper. Youlgreave in Derbyshire had only 200 inhabitants, but it had traditionally served a number of hamlets in that part of the Peak District, so in 1881 it had as many as four shopkeepers, a grocer and a baker.

Late 19th-century candle mould.

Inside a village shop, 1875.

A set of Typhoo tea cards, 'Work on the Farm', issued in the 1920s. On the back of the cards was a cheap offer for tennis balls.

It would be misleading to suggest that there was an abrupt change in the character of village shops. The nineteenth-century grocer kept items of drapery in stock, just as the seventeenth-century mercer had sold soap and spices. But by 1850 few retailers traded solely as mercers, drapers or tallow chandlers, and the fact that the leading retailers of a village tended to trade as grocers and general shopkeepers indicated a substantial change in the shopping habits of country people. More people were coming to the village shop for basic groceries and household goods, and the shopkeeper's trade was no longer confined to the spices, anchovies and silks that only the wealthy could afford. Now tea, coffee, sugar and black leading, for example, were being bought by all members of village society, rich or poor.

15

Fry's chocolate paste pot, 1853-54.

19th-century Horniman tea label. Horniman started selling tea in packets in 1826, at first via pedlars because grocers and shopkeepers were reluctant to stock a product that competed directly with their own blend.

Half-pound at 3s 4d **1s. 8d.**
HORNIMAN'S
PURE mixed TEA
the BLACK is <u>not</u> artificially colored,
the GREEN is a natural <u>dark olive</u> leaf,
<u>not</u> covered with the usual bluish powder.

"Tea costs the public annually twelve millions sterling, therefore its purity and reliable quality claims consideration."
House of Commons' Report on Tea.

*G*REAT STRENGTH combined with *fine flavour* is indispensable in tea, to obtain this all know that *young* leaves must alone be infused: *therefore Horniman & Co. import their tea NOT disguised with the usual colouring powder.* The *Times* in a leading article, August 15th, regrets that importers generally, to obtain extra gain, continue to encourage the Chinese to cover with mineral colour an article of daily consumption, so that inferior wintry leaves are made to counterfeit the best tea, and be passed off to the loss of the British consumer.

The extensive demand for Horniman's Tea, proves that the public appreciate its fine flavour, purity and great strength; therefore to enable purchasers to *identify this tea*, it is necessarily sold *only in packets*—never loose—the label is always signed *Horniman&Co* LONDON.
29,30,31 & 32, *Wormwood St., City.—Wholesale.*
CHEMISTS, CONFECTIONERS or BOOKSELLERS are AGENTS in all parts of the kingdom

An abundant supply of goods made possible by improvements in transport had much to do with this. Rural isolation and with it, self-sufficiency, were steadily eroded as new turnpike roads, canals, and railways in turn brought the products of industry and of overseas farming ever more cheaply, speedily and with greater regularity to all parts of the country. Tea, which had been a luxury, its price kept high by heavy excise duties, had by the early nineteenth century more than halved in price to between three and four shillings a pound retail for the cheaper varieties. It was now cheap enough for labourers to be including tea in their basic diet, much to the disgust of traditionalists like William Cobbett, who complained that tea-drinking was destroying the sturdiness of the English countryman.

As the nineteenth century progressed, the range of new processed groceries such as Huntley & Palmer's biscuits, Cadbury's chocolates and Pear's soap steadily increased, and the products were sold at low enough prices to ensure that they were accessible to a wide market. The same was true of manufactured goods, such as cheap, industrially produced wares from the Staffordshire potteries, Sheffield cutlery works and Lancashire cotton mills.

The effect on the village shopkeeper's trade was that the range of people from whom he drew his custom widened. At the end of the seventeenth century his trade had been confined almost entirely to the wealthy. By the end of the eighteenth century, rising standards of living among farmers had brought more of the middling and small farmers to the shopkeeper, and by the middle of the nineteenth century he had largely taken over the custom of the cottage people from the pedlars. By this time, the itinerants were unable to compete with the shopkeepers who could now receive regular deliveries of goods all year round.

The gentry continued to do their shopping in the village, often feeling impelled to support the tradesmen local to their estate. Where there was more than one similar shop, the landlords believed in being even-handed, dividing their purchasing more or less equally. The middling ranks – the vicar, the doctor, the leading farmers – aped this custom. Miss Lane, the postmistress at Flora Thompson's Candleford Green, bought from two bakers, one delivering one week, the other the next. The whole village gained from this custom of patronising local shops. The shopkeeper was able to maintain reasonably large stocks, including the premium groceries which earned him a healthy return and enabled him to be more accommodating towards his less well-off customers. Some shops were necessarily excluded from the gentry's custom: the poor widow who sold a few home-made sweets to the children, for example. At Candleford Green there was the dress shop of the Misses Pratt, whose goods were too dear for the poor and of insufficient quality to attract the rich.

Some indication of the nature of a mid-nineteenth-century village shopkeeper's business is revealed in the accounts kept by Edward Allnatt of Sonning in Berkshire in the 1860s. According to the county directories he was a grocer and baker, and his ledger amply confirms that. Bread features strongly in the sales. Cake is mentioned quite infrequently with no indication of what type was sold, except that some customers paid as much as a shilling, which must have bought a fair-sized cake. All the ingredients for baking were sold – flour and yeast, oatmeal,

Road wagon of the 1830s.

17

Ladies' sleeves, collars and buttons from Dorset and Kent, worn between the 1870s and 1900s.

baking powder, currants – sometimes in large quantities to farm households. One customer in particular regularly bought three or four gallons of flour, for which he paid about 3s 4d. The full range of groceries made up the bulk of Mr Allnatt's trade: tea, coffee (an ounce for five farthings), sugar, butter at 7d for half a pound and eggs for three farthings each. He sold a lot of bacon and pork, some fruit, mainly imports such as oranges and lemons, and sweets for the children. There was bird seed for the canary, and household items, such as washing blue, black leading, starch and matches. And then there was coal, for Mr Allnatt was evidently a coal merchant as well, with sales of five hundredweight of 'Forest Coal' (probably from the Forest of Dean) for 5s 6d – 6s being entered regularly in the ledger.

Apart from the coal, Mr Allnatt concentrated almost exclusively on his trade as grocer and baker. Other rural shopkeepers were less restrained and apparently

Top: Spoon for measuring out dry goods, such as grain or rice, probably 19th century. *Above:* Baker's delivery basket.

offered the villagers everything under the sun. 'Department stores in miniature' is how Dr Michael Winstanley has aptly described such shops. The principal line added to the grocery was usually drapery, providing a wide range of cottons, cords, calicoes, flannels, linens and other materials needed for making and mending clothes at home. There was little ready-made clothing before the end of the nineteenth century, and thick, striped shirting material tended to have a steady sale, for all the farmworkers wore shirts made of this hard-wearing fabric. Most items of haberdashery were kept in stock, including ribbons and lace for trimmings, crêpe for mourning, hat pins, sewing threads, wool for darning socks, needles and pins, hooks and eyes, and buttons. The detachable collars for men's shirts were usually kept by the village shop, and some also carried thick corduroy trousers. Leather gloves worn for hedging and ditching work, and cloth caps were regularly sold, while for the women there were white pinafores, silk stockings and muffs. By the end of the nineteenth century, village shops were often keeping stocks of boots and shoes, as factory-made products began to displace the footwear made by the country shoemaker.

The shop of a general village shopkeeper was usually divided down the middle, with a grocery counter on one side and a drapery counter piled high with different fabrics on the other. George Starr, who kept shop at Cley in Norfolk,

Gentleman's tie, collar and cravat from Dorset and Kent worn between the 1870s and 1900.

19

THOMAS AARON TILLOTT,

Draper, Grocer; Tea, Flour, and Provision Dealer, etc

READY-MADE CLOTHING.

BOOTS & SHOES, BRUSHES, MATS, AND FARMER.

ALL GOODS DELIVERED DAILY, ANY DISTANCE, CARRIAGE PAID.
CHARGES ARE MOST MODERATE.

WHITE HART STREET, EAST HARLING, THETFORD, NORFOLK

Advertisement in *Kelly's Directory of Norfolk*, 1892, which shows the range of activities undertaken by a late 19th-century retailer.

was among those fortunate enough to have a sizeable building enabling him to have a small drapery showroom where fabrics, hats and clothes could be displayed. Behind the shop he possessed two old malthouses in which he kept his additional stocks of draperies and groceries. Other shops which developed into general emporia had upstairs rooms or expanded into a neighbouring cottage where lino, crockery, ironmongery, garden tools and seeds would be sold.

The post office was often an important adjunct to a village shop's business. However, the combination of shop and post office was not as usual in the mid-nineteenth century as it was later to become. When village post offices were

A country butcher at Haddenham, Buckinghamshire, in about 1900, continuing the traditional practice of buying fatstock direct from market.

Hambleden, Buckinghamshire, in 1907, with its shop opposite the village pump.

becoming established between the 1840s and 1860s the occupations of those entrusted with the handling of the Royal Mail varied quite widely. Miss Lane at Candleford Green had a blacksmith's and wheelwright's business. Farmers, shoemakers and tailors were among those who held the post office contract, while for others it was their sole occupation. Less than half the village post offices in the 1850s were in the hands of grocers and shopkeepers, but gradually more post office contracts were awarded to shopkeepers, and more wheelwrights, blacksmiths and so on took up retailing alongside the post office business.

Besides the general stores, there were a few more specialist retailers. Butchers and bakers were the most common, to be found even in quite small villages of no more than 200 inhabitants. Both continued to be as much producers as retailers, baking their own bread or butchering fatstock bought ready for slaughter. Large villages were able to support other specialist shops. Chemists and druggists were quite common, drawing their custom mainly from the better-off who could afford the medical preparations they stocked. In the Lincolnshire village of Corby, there was a chemist who was also a wine merchant, a not unusual combination of trades, resulting perhaps from the fact that chemists naturally tended to stock a wide range of 'tonic' wines. It was a combination that lasted well into

the twentieth century before off-licences became a more usual part of a grocer's business. In some villages there was an ironmonger's shop, though as often as not it was a part-time addition to a blacksmith's or wheelwright's business. Stationers, confectioners and china and glass dealers were also to be found occasionally. Eynsham, one of Oxfordshire's largest villages, had in the 1860s and 1870s almost as full a range of retail services as any village could support. Even so, it was the general retailers that were dominant.

Most of the retail trade of the village passed through the small number of substantial grocery and general stores. Even in large villages there was only enough business to support one or two of these. At Corsley, Wiltshire, where the population exceeded 800 at the end of the nineteenth century, only one of the three general stores could be described as doing good business. In Corby, Lincolnshire, another settlement of reasonable size, Willerton's stores was dominant amongst local retailers from the mid-nineteenth century for more than a hundred years. R.T. Willerton opened his shop in 1842 and it is clear from the advertisements for his draperies placed in the local *Grantham Journal* that he was soon trying to attract custom from surrounding villages. In these advertisements he described himself as draper, mercer and hatter, but he was also established as a grocer as well as having received the local post office contract.

There was nothing of the quaint or unbusinesslike about these shops. Their opening hours were regular and long – many shops stayed open until 7 or 8 o'clock most days of the week. On Saturday, when well over half the week's income came in, closing time could be as late as 11 o'clock, and the same was usual for a few days before Christmas. The large general stores were among the leading employers in the village. Two or three counter assistants, a delivery boy or two, and a general hand to work in the storeroom meant that a shop could have half a dozen employees or more, and that outdid most village businesses.

The other shops, those which could not be described as doing good business, were as often as not part-time occupations. Farmers, market gardeners, publicans, carriers, wholesale dealers and brewers were among those who kept a shop as a sideline. Numerous spinsters and widows eked out some sort of living from small shops. Trading methods in these establishments tended to be more casual than those in the more orderly, larger stores. Intending customers for Miss Hannah's shop at Cley, Norfolk, had first to call at the cottage to fetch her out to open the shop a few yards down the road. At Bishopsbourne in Kent, where an old lady kept shop in her cottage, shoppers waited in the front room while the things they asked for were fetched through from the back. On Saturday night the shop's trappings were pushed aside, and the front room, complete with piano moved into its centre, was converted to a parlour for the weekend.

While the small and part-time businesses tended to be ephemeral, dying with their owners, the larger village stores were passed on to the next generation, often remaining in the same family. William Allnatt succeeded Edward as grocer and baker in Sonning and maintained the business throughout the 1920s and 1930s. R.T. Willerton in Corby was followed by his son Henry, who enlarged the business during the twentieth century by opening branches in nearby villages.

Beer retailer, who, unlike a publican, could not sell beer for consumption on the premises.

The co-operative stores in the main street of the village of Aldermaston, Berkshire, 1911.

One-man and family businesses predominated, but there were some village shops that were run by co-operative societies. Most of these were in villages that had strong associations with industry – they were either close to industrial towns or had their own large industry, as was the case in coal-mining districts from Northumberland to Somerset. The shop at Peak Forest in Derbyshire, where quarrying for lime was an important business, was organised by a co-operative society. The leather and shoemaking trades were important parts of the economy of Long Buckby, a large village in Northamptonshire, and a co-operative society was founded here in the 1860s. Oakhill, Somerset, which had a 'Co-operative Stores', was a village of moderate size with a population in 1901 of 434, where the principal employer was the large brewery. However, there were some villages in which co-operative stores operated where there were no such dominant industries. Evershot and Child Okeford, two large villages in Dorset, each had a local co-operative society. In Ardington, Berkshire, a co-operative store was founded in 1885 by Lord Wantage, the local landowner, largely out of philanthropic motives, to encourage thrift amongst the villagers.

Little of the village shopkeeper's trade at this time was in ready-prepared and packaged goods supplied by manufacturers and wholesalers. Mr Allnatt's ledger

Staff at the Oakhill Co-operative Society's store in Somerset showing off their range of bread and cakes.

records sales of 'biscuits' and it is clear from the varied weights and prices that these were bought wholesale and sold loose. The major biscuit makers, such as Huntley & Palmer and Peek Frean, had supplied 1 lb and 2 lb assortments in tins since the late 1830s, but it was only at Christmas time that the village shopkeeper had much trade in them. Then he was likely to fill his window with a special display of the gaily coloured tins. A few other items were supplied in boxes, bottles or jars. Some ginger-beer makers delivered their product in earthenware bottles; glass jars were used for pickles, and matches, invented in 1826, were sold in boxes or in upright tins containing a hundred.

For the most part, however, the grocer of the eighteenth and nineteenth centuries bought wholesale consignments – sacks of flour and oatmeal, barrels of vinegar and dried fruit, chests of tea. Sugar was supplied as a solid cone of 'loaf sugar' which had to be cut into the ounces and pounds which villagers wanted to buy – a laborious task. Salt also arrived in a large block, and soap came as a slab about eighteen inches long to be sliced into one-pound bars. Dried fruit had to be cleaned, by being rubbed through sieves, though brushing machines were available to do most of the work by the late nineteenth century. Bacon was sliced by hand, coffee was ground, and tea blended. Tea-blending was often a matter

of some pride, with the proprietor creating a special blend of tea to suit the local water and often giving it prominent advertisement. In the smaller shops, the blending was likely to be a rather haphazard undertaking.

Most of the groceries were sold by weight, though shopkeepers often fell short of the rigours of modern trading standards. It was common to sell goods by gross weight, inclusive of the wrappings. The grocer could buy paper bags pre-printed with specific weights, and usually used blue bags for sugar, yellow for dried fruit and white or brown for other goods. In country shops, the use of local weights and measures lingered on late into the nineteenth century, well after the imperial standard had become general in almost all other walks of life. Some goods were sold by measure: flour by the gallon, bran and oatmeal by the

The marble-stoppered bottle for mineral waters, devised by Hiram Codd in 1875, was common in the late 19th century and survived into the 1920s. Screw-topped bottles of the type seen second from the right were regularly used from the 1890s; on the right is a plain medicine bottle.

bushel. For small purchases, though, the villager was more likely to bring a tin, bottle or jar to be filled with a pennyworth of tea or vinegar or treacle.

Credit played an important part in the village shopkeeper's trade. The squires, farmers and the other tradesmen rarely paid cash, buying instead on account and settling once every month or six weeks. Fortunately for the shopkeeper's peace of mind most did so, but it was not uncommon to have to wait a year or more for payment from the squire who expected to be asked at least twice for bills to be settled, or from the farmer who was perpetually in need of a good day at the market to pay his accounts. At Sonning in Berkshire, Edward Allnatt's ledger at the end of 1866 included bills which had been outstanding for three years.

It was the same with the poor, except that they did not have unsettled accounts, they simply had debt. Labourers, smallholders and small-time tradesmen all found it easy to slip into debt with the shopkeeper, even on quite minimal purchases of tea, sugar, starch and soap. Once incurred, it could take years for debts to be cleared. A labourer in a Devon village ended 1895 with a debt of £2 18s to the shopkeeper. A year later this had grown to £6 6s 6d. Irregular payments

While beers, wines and mineral waters were commonly supplied in glass bottles by about 1850; vinegar and ginger beer were still supplied in stoneware bottles into the 20th century. New household products such as ink and paste were also sold in stoneware containers. From the 1890s bottles often had transfer-printed labels, although these ginger beer containers have not.

Opposite page. Top left: Spring balance scales, used to weigh all sorts of produce in a wide variety of shops. The larger hook dealt with heavy weights graduated from 20 to 300 lbs. The small hook, situated at a point where the balance could be more easily forced apart, was for smaller weights – up to 40 lbs. *Top right:* Free sample tin of Huntley & Palmers ginger nuts, made between 1900 and 1914, showing the biscuit factory in Reading. 1lb and 2lb tins were of similar design. *Bottom left:* Late 19th-century metal can, green with gold lettering and brass taps, used by a grocer for metering out treacle. *Bottom right:* Sugar cutters from a grocer's shop, second half of 19th century. Loaf sugar, arriving in 'titlers' or awkwardly shaped loaves, had to be cut up before sale.

Right: A Christmas-tide display of bisuits. *Below:* Bushel measure for grain, made in Norwich during the reign of Victoria.

were made during 1897, enough to bring the total owing down to £4 10s, but it was not until 1911 that this man was completely free of debt. His plight was by no means the worst. There was a smallholder who had built up a debt with this same shop during 1895 of £9 10s. He, too, made a number of small occasional payments during succeeding years, resorting to barter on occasions – his potato crop of 1896 went to the shopkeeper. He stopped making purchases at this shop, but the debt was not finally cleared until 1915.

Top left: 19th-century measures – gallon, half-gallon and quart. *Top right:* Tea-packeting moulds. After Horniman started selling tea by net weight in the 1820s, other grocers were forced to follow his lead. Brown paper bags, sealed at the base, were placed in the mould, and the wooden plunger forced them into packet shape. *Bottom left:* A set of nesting weights, probably 19th century.

Shopkeepers simply accepted the inability of the poor to meet any but the smallest debt, and there were some like Mrs Tarman at Candleford Green who treated the cottage folk with considerable indulgence: 'Many a cooked ham-bone with good picking still left on it and many a hock-end of bacon were slipped by her into the shopping baskets of poor mothers of families' (Flora Thompson, *Lark Rise to Candleford*). Undoubtedly the security of the trade from the middle classes and gentry underwrote such generosity. But the period when the village shop had such a strong place in village life, serving all its members, both rich and poor, proved to be short-lived. Even at the time of which Flora Thompson wrote, the 1880s, the outward spread of urban values was introducing new competition which was ultimately to weaken the village shop.

Above: Interior of a shop at Shere, Surrey, 1885.
Right: Victorian tobacco jars of painted stoneware. On one, the inscription 'Digger Flake' can still be made out. Until cigarettes became popular, tobacco was cut and weighed to each customer's order.

Challenges: 1880-1940

Opposite: The sweet shop at Prittlewell, Essex, c.1891.

The staff of Brimpton stores, Berkshire, in 1908. In a village of 400 inhabitants, this shop offered a good range of carpets, lino, baskets, galvanised iron buckets and ornamental china.

As far as outward appearance was concerned, the village shop of 1940 was little changed from that of 1880. Descriptions written in the 1920s and 1930s emphasise characteristics already observed in the Victorian period, with shops selling a wide range of groceries, household goods and drapery. Methods of trading were unchanged: goods were variously weighed out, cut up, sliced and bundled up for customers while they waited, and people still brought jars and bottles for their pennyworths of golden syrup or vinegar. While accurate in some

Clarke's Pyramid Night Lights. Night lights, which were squat candles designed to burn for up to ten hours, became popular during the late 19th century.

Inside a small village shop in the 1930s. The stock was not large and although there are some individually packaged and processed items, such as Shredded Wheat, the drawers, large tins and Golden Syrup dispenser show that much was still sold loose. The barrel and stool provided some comfort for the customers as they passed the time of day while their orders were made up.

respects, this vision of unchanging rural charm was misleading as it overlooked factors which had caused some rapid changes in the character of village shops.

The fiercest challenge faced by the village shop arose from the strengthening competition presented by the traders in market towns, and later by distant firms selling by mail order. Such competition had always existed – people had long been attracted to the variety of choice offered by markets and shops in towns, with even the poor being prepared to walk several miles on a Saturday afternoon. The village shop had originally become established as a result of improved transport which brought regular supplies and more trade at the expense of the hawkers. But by the end of the nineteenth century, continuing improvements in communications were bringing the town's shops into more direct competition with those of the village. At the same time incomes and standards of living were rising, and people began to spend more of their money on the luxury items that a small village shopkeeper could not afford to keep in stock. Nationally advertised branded goods, obtainable mainly through chain stores, also drew people into the market towns, and once there, they tended to do the rest of their household shopping in town rather than in the village.

One of the first developments in transport at this time was the growth of local carrier services from village to town. Every market day, the carrier would set off from the village early in the morning and drive his wagon or van at an ambling pace into town, setting off again in the mid-afternoon to be back home early in the evening. The number of these services increased substantially during the second half of the nineteenth century, especially those running into the larger market towns. Services to Guildford, for example, increased from 106 in 1854 to 166 in 1914. More villages were served by carriers than before, and more villagers could avail themselves of a cheap, if rather uncomfortable ride to market. All the same, the most capacious of carriers' wagons could take no more than fifteen or so people packed rather tightly, so this by no means covered all the village shopkeeper's clientele. But the carrier also acted as shopping agent for those who were not making the journey. Villagers would hand over their

Top: A simple wooden device for holding balls of string. *Above:* 19th-century pair of scales, made by J. Wilder of Reading, and used for many years in a village shop in Berkshire. *Right:* A Rowntree's chocolate tin commemorating the coronation of Edward VII.

Austin's stores at Eastry, Kent, comprising some four departments in two buildings.

shopping lists to be discharged by the carrier during the three or four hours' stay in the town, and he would return laden with parcels of groceries, joints of meat, medicines, clothes, shoes, saucepans and kettles, all somehow fitted into the van between and around the passengers. Villagers paid the carrier a penny or two for this service, considered by many well worthwhile in view of the wider range of cheaper goods available in the towns.

Some carriers offered additional services. One at Waltham, in Kent, for example, would bring goods on approval (shoes in particular) from the shops in Canterbury. In Somerset Maugham's *Cakes and Ale*, one of the things brought back to the village by the carrier was a bicycle – a sign of the greater mobility that was coming to the countryside. Villagers began to use bicycles for shopping excursions to the nearest town – a round trip of ten or more miles was readily accepted as within reasonable pedalling distance. Motor cars and motorcycles, which offered still greater opportunities for shopping farther afield, soon followed, although by the end of the 1930s ownership of cars by country people was still largely confined to the gentry, farmers, the better-off tradesmen and

Carrier's Van.

A light-running Van, on springs and patent axles, body 7 ft. by 4 ft., inside measure, to carry 15 to 20 cwt., dripples with hinged seatboards and portable backs to seats, door at back, boarded top, glass lights in sides and back, portable seat at front with curtains behind same, guard rail round roof, step at back, hay cratch, and American cloth cushions to seats.

£65 0 0.

Extras, if required :—
Pole for two horses, £2 0 0.
Break, £3 0 0.
Lamps, 20/- to 30/-.

Carrier's van, 1907.

Above: Wooden butter scales, from Buckinghamshire, and probably used in a shop selling dairy produce. The central pillar is made of beech and the pans of sycamore, suspended by twisted lengths of cord. *Right:* The village shop at Peasmarsh, near Rye in Kent, early this century, divided into drapery and grocery departments.

professional classes – those who would previously have had their own horse-drawn transport. Even so, the loss of the custom of this section of society had a considerable effect on the village shop.

The motor bus had an even greater impact. The first services began running in 1898, and over the next fifteen years several rural routes were established,

By the time this photograph was taken in the early 1900s, Midsomer Norton, in the coal-mining area of Somerset, was a distinctly over-sized village, and one of its leading shops had acquired urban-style premises. Yet its trade remained that of the village store, combining grocery, drapery, ironmongery and patent medicines.

The post office and general stores at Eastbury, near Newbury, Berkshire, in about 1907.

often by railway companies who used the buses as feeders to their lines. Motor buses provided a more frequent and faster service into town than the carrier's van and could carry three or four times as many passengers. Between 1918 and 1930 country bus services expanded rapidly, and a dense network was created by a combination of local operators and large regional companies. The traditional carriers were of course affected by the new bus services, although many followed their example and bought motor vehicles to use on the old market-day routes through the villages with stops at farms and businesses on the way.

It was not, however, only transport services that drew people away. The shops in the towns held great attractions: goods were likely to be cheaper, especially on the market stalls, and the chain stores that were steadily taking over the market town's high street – the Lipton and Maypole grocery stores, the Stead & Simpson shoe shops, Boots the Chemist and Woolworth's fancy bazaars – were the trendsetters of retailing, selling the well-known brands and the most up-to-date and fashionable goods. By the 1920s and 1930s, radio broadcasting and

Above: Oil cycle lamp made by the firm of Joseph Lucas of Birmingham in about 1895. *Top right:* The post office and stores at Ecchinswell, Hampshire, which also ran a bicycle sales and repair business, c.1906-10. *Bottom right:* The village shop at Ightham, Kent, c.1901. *Below:* Advertisement for boot polish, 1910.

cheap, popular newspapers had made even the most far-flung countrymen aware of the new range of consumer goods available. Since it took only an hour to travel twenty miles by bus, many people began not just to travel to the market towns but to pay at least an occasional visit to the main towns of the county where the chain stores and department stores were bigger and had even more to offer.

As well as attracting people away from the village shop, more and more town shops began to provide delivery services to the villages. At first, these were horse-drawn vans. For example, in about 1900, a grocer in Canterbury started sending a van to Ickham, five miles away, delivering candles, paraffin oil and groceries at prices lower than those charged by the village shop. After the First World War, motor vans became more common and the variety of deliveries and services available at a distance from the market town became wider. For instance, one of the drapers in Chesham, Buckinghamshire, at this time ran a clothing club, which involved sending someone round the villages to collect payments and deliver purchases. Far sterner competition than this, however, was to face village drapery stores in the inter-war period, and it came from the mail-order companies who had begun to despatch cheap, reasonably fashionable readymade clothing from warehouses in Manchester direct to the customer.

Yet another problem facing country shopkeepers was the decline in village populations. The depopulation of the countryside had been under way since the middle of the nineteenth century as increasing numbers moved to the towns in pursuit of jobs in industry. By 1861 the migration was already strong enough for some predominantly rural counties such as Wiltshire and Norfolk to show a decline in population, and by 1900 no region in England could be said to be immune to the trend.

The combined effect of declining population and competition from outside was at first to arrest the increase in numbers of village shops and before long actually to send them into decline. It was the small villages, those with fewer than 500 inhabitants, that were the hardest hit. It was not unusual for there to be fewer shops in these villages in 1940 than there had been in 1900. In the North Riding of Yorkshire, Kilburn had three shopkeepers entered in the directory for 1909, but by 1933 there was just one butcher. Stapleford, in Wiltshire, a village of 247 inhabitants in 1901, then supported a butcher, a baker-cum-grocer and a general shop, but by the 1930s the population was down to 215, and the general shop had gone. Some small villages lost all their shops: Chesterton, a Warwickshire village, declined in population from 192 in 1891 when there were two shops to 135 in 1931 when there were none.

Darlington Market, County Durham, 1920s.

Above: Mr Charlie Merritt with Savage & Parsons delivery cart, East Meon, Hampshire. This photograph indicates the development of the roundsman system and the decline of home-baking. *Top right:* The village baker in Corringham, Essex, takes to motor transport, 1920s. *Bottom right:* Luxborough Post Office, Somerset, early 20th century.

In some of the larger villages, the whole range of retailers survived. In Yorkshire, shopkeepers left Kilburn, but only five miles away the village of Ampleforth, which was a centre for its immediate locality, lost none of its shops. Other villages of comparable size were not so lucky. In the Lincolnshire village of Corby, the twenty retail outlets of 1872 had become sixteen by 1905 and fourteen by 1937. Avebury, a Wiltshire village of nearly 600 inhabitants in 1901, with four shops and two grocers, had just a grocer, a baker and a shopkeeper by 1935.

Almost all village shopkeepers had to find ways of meeting the changing demands of the market – or indeed meet the competition head on if they were not to lose their business to the town.

When at the turn of the century the grocer from Canterbury began to send his delivery cart round the villages, the response of Charles Coombs, owner of

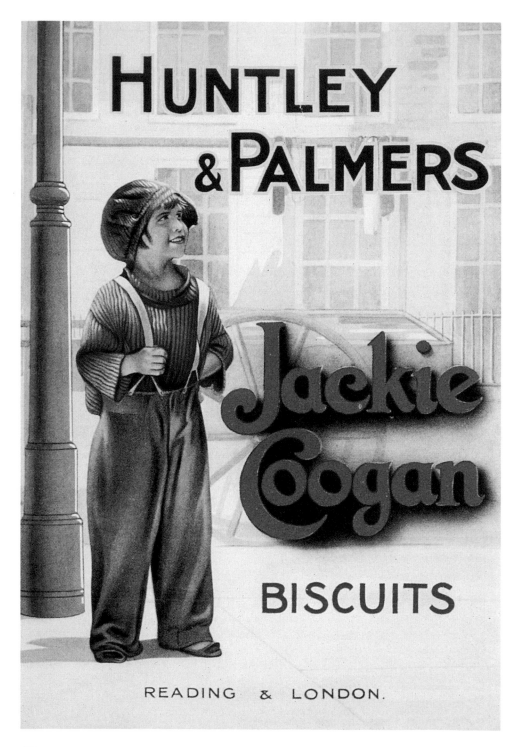

Biscuits named after the child star in Charles Chaplin's film *The Kid* (1921).

Polish, 1930s.

the village shop at Ickham, was to buy a bicycle so that he could tour the village delivering paraffin oil. This fairly drastic action was prompted by a dramatic fall in his takings after the city grocer appeared on the scene. But his enterprise paid off and in 1915 he bought a motorcycle and after the war a motor van as he extended his deliveries to other villages within a five-mile radius of Ickham.

Some of the ways in which customers were encouraged to keep their business in the village were not new. Clothing clubs, for example, in existence since the middle of the nineteenth century were self-help organisations through which labourers could save for expensive items such as clothes, shoes and bedding. Shopkeepers later began to organise their own clubs as a means of developing customer loyalty. At Cley, in Norfolk, members paid an agreed amount to George Starr the shopkeeper each week, and at the year's end he rewarded those who had kept up payments regularly with a small bonus. This was an occasion of some little ceremony, with the customer being made quite a fuss of as she cashed in her card on the clothing of her choice. As well as clothing clubs, there were Christmas clubs and sometimes a children's club which all guaranteed at least some trade for the shop.

Those shopkeepers who were also village postmasters found the post office playing an increasingly important part in their business. The amount of official business was growing as new tasks such as the payment of old age pensions were given to the post office, which meant that income from the post office contract was rising. Just as valuable, however, was the fact that people coming in for a few stamps, to send a telegram or to collect a pension were likely to be drawn into making other purchases while they happened to be in the shop.

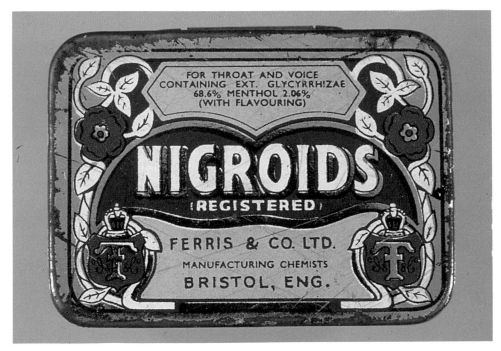

Early 20th-century cough sweets tin.

Soon the new consumer goods industries, which were making the fortunes of the chain stores and department stores in town, were having an impact on the stocks held in the village shop. Villagers who in earlier times would have asked for half a gallon of oatmeal now preferred a packet of porridge oats. More and more shelves in the village shop were filled with goods supplied by manufacturers or wholesalers in packets, jars or tins, many of which were branded and often heavily advertised. By the 1870s and 1880s several products had national distribution. Almost every newspaper in the country carried advertisements for Epps's cocoa, and enamel signs promoting it were erected at even the smallest

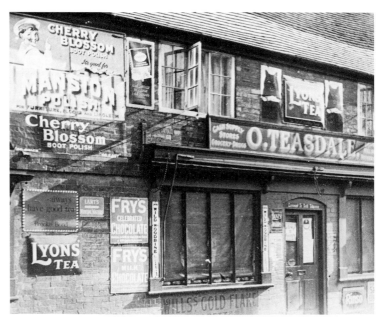

White cotton bandage with instructions (printed in black) which was part of the stock of George Senior, a chemist in Holsworthy, Devon; it probably dates from c.1910 or slightly later.

Opposite. Top left: Alfred Dean's shop at Newdigate, Surrey, photographed at about the time the advertisement of branded goods was becoming common (1880s and 1890s), with advertised items well to the fore in the window. *Top right:* Advertisement from an 1880s trade directory. *Bottom left:* The combined grocery store and post office at East Clandon, Surrey, c.1910. *Bottom right:* A shop in Wolston, Leicestershire, in the 1930s, its walls devoted to advertisements, some of which recall products that have long since disappeared.

of wayside railway stations. Rival products manufactured by Fry's and Cadbury's were given similar treatment – white lettering arranged in a semi-circle and spelling out 'Cadbury's chocolate' soon adorned shop windows in villages up and down the land. By 1910, products such as Colman's mustards, Mazawattee tea, Crosse & Blackwell sauces, Cerebos salt, Nestle's condensed milk and Pear's and Hudson's soaps were prominently featured in the village shop's stock, and the shop began to fill with enamel signs and posters advertising these wares. The inter-war years added varieties of breakfast cereals, jellies and blancmanges, tinned vegetables and fruit, and detergents and cleaning agents to the range of packeted and branded goods on the shopkeeper's shelves. There were dairy products as well: the first packets of Anchor butter, in 1lb cartons, went on sale in London in 1924, and during the next decade it reached the village shops.

A pre-World War I advertisement placed by a Surrey shopkeeper in his parish magazine to promote the attractions of shopping locally in preference to visiting the towns.

WHY? Go to Dorking, London, or elsewhere for

Grocery, Drapery, Clothing (*Ready-made or to measure*), Hats, Boots, Ironmongery, Earthenware, Garden Tools, etc., etc.

When you can obtain them on best terms at

ALFRED DEAN'S

GENERAL ⚬ SUPPLY ⚬ STORES, NEWDIGATE.

ANY ARTICLE NOT IN STOCK PROCURED ON SHORT NOTICE.

The selling of branded goods had a number of advantages for village shop-keepers. They benefited from heavy promotional advertising organised by the manufacturers for their products, which convinced people that they needed items they had not previously regarded as essential. In addition to this, many branded goods such as cigarettes and chocolate were items that people purchased quite regularly in small quantities, so the local village shop was as good a place as any to buy them. Resale price maintenance on branded products was introduced in the 1890s on a few items and after 1914 rapidly extended to cover a large number of the goods sold by village shops. Although the urban chain stores could still sell their own-label goods at lower prices than the major brands, the existence of price maintenance certainly acted as an encouragement to people to shop locally if they had no special need to go outside the village.

Selling packaged goods eliminated much of the work that had traditionally been part of the grocer's life, such as cutting up, weighing and bagging, though

By the late 19th century, pipe tobacco was sold in tins: Churchman's Honeydew Flake (*top left*) and Recorder Full Strength (*front left*). The metal tape measure is a promotional item distributed by a tobacco manufacturer. The Oxo tin dates from the 1930s.

Bovril advertisements dating from (*left*) 1903 and (*right*) 1915.

not all of it, for many things were still sold loose, among them rice, dried fruit and biscuits. Sugar was still weighed out into the blue bags, coffee had to be ground, and bacon was sliced. Even here, though, there were changes. Bacon-slicing machines, installed by many village shops in the 1920s and 1930s, made a considerable difference to the counter assistant's work. 'What a thrill it was, and how easy!' recalls Freda Starr of her father's bacon slicer bought in 1926. 'Charlie [the general assistant] took great pride in looking after it and keeping it well oiled and spotlessly clean.' Among his sketches of rural life in Yorkshire, J. Fairfax-Blakeborough gives an account of a villager who advised tourists looking for local sights to go down to the village shop and see the wonderful new slicing machine.

BOB GOES ON SEARCHING.

"SOMEWHERE IN ENGLAND"

DEAR READERS

ANOTHER DISAPPOINTMENT WAS IN STORE FOR ME IN MY SEARCH FOR **Ye Olde Englishe Shoppe.**

ALAS IT HAS BEEN SADLY RE-STORED

DEJECTEDLY YOURS
BOB

By 1930, the village shopkeeper's efforts to move with the times were attracting satirical comment from those in search of rural charm. From *The Leicester Mail*, 2nd September 1930.

Other social changes had their effect on village shops. Universal literacy produced a demand for reading matter and a wide variety of popular newspapers and magazines was founded between 1880 and 1940, ranging from the *Daily Mail, Woman's Weekly* and *Meccano Magazine* to *Comic Cuts* and *Radio Fun*. Selling newspapers and magazines represented a steady trade which for many a general village store became a valued support to its other lines. There were also considerable numbers of shops which were primarily newsagents but also stocked sweets, tobacco, toys and fancy goods. Some were new business ventures, others had previously been other businesses but had taken on the selling of newspapers as their main activity.

Greengrocers also became more common in villages, having been a relatively rare sight in the nineteenth century, when people either grew their own vegetables in their gardens or bought from friends or a local smallholder. The same had been true of fruit, with the village store usually selling only imported fruit such as oranges and lemons. Even in areas like Kent, where fruit was grown on a large scale, it was almost unobtainable in local shops. Benjamin Harrison who

A small newsagent at Aylestone, Leicestershire,
between the world wars.

Dorset village shop, 1927.

Top left: Catering to the tourist trade in 1939. A farm-produce shop at Weston Subedge, Gloucestershire. *Bottom left:* Branded groceries of the inter-war years with one of the ornate cash registers of the time. *Above:* Packaging in World War II – the partial label saved paper.

Left: Mrs Qualtrough in her village shop at St John's, County Durham, c.1935. *Right:* General stores, 1940s.

kept a shop at Ightham in Kent recorded in his diary in 1903, 'Two young cyclists came in and asked whether I could tell them where they could get some cherries or other fruit. Alas, I could not. One of them was a splendid sort. She said, "It is so tantalising to see the fruit as we ride along and yet be unable to buy any." '

Catering for the growing tourist trade in rural areas was one of the factors which brought fresh fruit and vegetables into village shops. In some of the more popular areas, a few farm-produce shops were opened specifically for the holiday trade in the 1930s. Local village trade in greengrocery was also expanding. People were both eating more fruit and vegetables and tending to become less self-sufficient, and began to supplement, or even replace, what they would previously have grown in their gardens. In most villages the general store handled the sale of fruit and vegetables, but in larger places there might be someone trading as greengrocer or fruiterer.

The example of Henry Willerton, who opened his little chain of stores in the village around Corby in the interwar years and made a good living shows that it was possible to succeed in village shopkeeping in spite of the challenges presented by the times. And there were many other examples of similar success scattered across the country. But certain problems remained that did not augur well for the future. Most important was the fact that village shopkeepers were ceasing to serve the whole village in the way that they had done in the mid-Victorian

A survivor: a shop at Clun, Shropshire, photographed in the 1960s, but with relatively little to suggest that it does not date from fifty years earlier.

period. The gentry now rarely shopped in the village. In many places, estates had been broken up and the landowners had moved away, but even where they remained a loosening of social ties meant that the gentry no longer felt any obligation to buy locally. Many of the farmers, professional people and other tradesmen of the village had acquired cars, and their wives had the time andmoney to make a bus journey into town once a week. Increasingly the village shopkeeper was drawing his custom from the poor and the immobile. In the short term this was perhaps of little importance. According to Francis Brett Young, whose *Portrait of a Village* was written in the 1930s, Mr Cantlow, a shopkeeper in Monk's Norton, Worcestershire, 'prefers to deal with the cottage-folk, who live from hand to mouth, who can only find cash for the necessaries of life on Saturdays, and are thankful to pay through the nose so long as he gives them credit'. In the long run, though, even ties of debt-ridden deference could be broken, forcing the shopkeeper to make greater efforts to attract customers.

The Second World War brought some respite from the pressures on the village shop. Rationing tied people to their local shop, while shortages of petrol meant that they could not travel so frequently to the market town. Some village shopkeepers were remarkably successful at finding supplies of unrationed goods, and at tapping local sources of eggs, cream and bacon, which were sold 'under the counter' to those prepared to pay a little extra. But most of the non-rationed goods tended to go to the shops in town, which encouraged people from the villages to make the journey whenever possible. It was a pattern that was to persist through the years of post-war rationing, and as mobility gradually became easier, so the pressures on village shopkeeping grew ever greater.

After 1945: Use It or Lose It

Ambridge village shop in the radio series 'The Archers' represents the popular conception of the village store – as much a social focus as the local inn, with a leisurely 'time for anything approach' that combines genuine neighbourliness with love of a good gossip. In the real world, however, it is very doubtful that the shop could be run economically, despite Jack Woolley's installation of a modern automated till. In fact, it would be lucky to survive. For the outstanding feature of rural retailing since the Second World War has been the decline of the village shop, as more and more proprietors have given up the unequal struggle to make ends meet.

It is a sign of the times when a pensioner is so delighted that her village has retained even one store that she writes a poem about it. Mrs Jessie Vernon, who is in her seventies and suffers from arthritis, penned these lines after seeing the improvements made to Ovingham village store when a new owner took over.

Mrs Vernon with her poem outside Ovingham village shop, Northumberland, September 1986.

A Poem in Praise of the Village Shop

For many years we have moaned and moaned –
No decent shop for food, we groaned,
Trudging the bridge to Prudhoe or Town
With bulging bags that weighed us down.

Hooray! hooray! what have we here?
A mini supermarket, that's very clear.
Nothing like this has our village seen –
You won't believe it unless you've been.
Shelves packed with goods from ceiling to floor,
Fridge units full of cold foods galore!
With a lovely carpet right through the door.

The young man who did this deserves our thanks,
Let's hope he takes full tills to the bank!
He will certainly need our village support
To ensure his shelves are never short.
As a pensioner whose shopping has been a chore,
This shop will be a boon to myself and more.

She adds: 'I thought he deserved some thanks from someone. He sells everything and it is fantastic. There are a lot of elderly people in Ovingham with no cars and we need a village shop. I hope people support it by shopping there.' (*The Journal*, Newcastle upon Tyne, 17th September 1986.)

To put actual figures on the decline of the village shop is difficult, as available statistics vary either in the size of settlement they refer to or in the year in which records start. In addition, figures do not exist for all counties, and different areas have almost certainly suffered in different degrees. From what is known, though, those mentioned below seem to have been among the worst affected.

By 1979, 44% of all villages in Dorset were without a shop and only 12% had more than one shop, while in Nottinghamshire, over 40% of villages in the county had no shop, and in the previous five years alone 10% of those villages with stores had lost them.

In Durham, the western parishes lost a total of 56 shops between 1972 and 1982 accounting for one in seven of all shops and many of those that survive are at risk.

In Norfolk, the number of food stores in rural districts fell by just over 600 between 1951 and 1980, and Suffolk villages lost no fewer than 137 general stores, 43 sub post offices, 82 pubs, 34 garages, 22 butchers and 19 baker's shops between 1961 and 1978.

Rural Wales was also severely affected. In Gwynedd, shop numbers dropped by 19% between 1972 and 1982, by which time 47% of all villages had no shop.

Andrew Lawson noted of this shop in Hartland, Devon, in 1976: 'Ruby Westland sells just about everything in her tiny village shop. She stocks sweets and stationery, tobacco and cycle spares, petrol and paraffin. Her father, a shoemaker, died in 1949, but she still sells shoes and Wellington boots, some of them with the wartime utility mark.'

Elsewhere the rate and extent of closure may have been less dramatic, but any village with a population of less than 500 is vulnerable, and recent research shows that the trend is continuing. Probably a quarter of all settlements of this size in England and Wales now have no general food store or sub post office and the percentage is considerably higher in Scotland. Mobile shops provide an important service in scattered communities, but the low margins of profit on groceries and the increasing cost of keeping vehicles on the road has led to a drop in numbers even since the 1970s, with further decline likely.

There are several important factors behind the disappearance of village shops, all of which were to some extent apparent before the Second World War, although the situation has certainly worsened since then. Firstly, there has been a steady loss of population from many rural districts, caused by farming becoming more mechanised and agricultural workers leaving the land to find new jobs in

The wooden pepper mill contains powder for dusting the feet of potential customers for shoes. the large wooden box contains string for wrapping parcels.

Village shop, Essex, 1970.

General stores, 1950s.

Left: The manager of the Stewkley co-operative stores in December 1967, Mr Donald Pullinger, dressing his window. *Right:* Village shop, Cowden, Kent, 1960s.

the towns and cities. By the 1950s, too, the old country trades had virtually disappeared and few successful businesses were established to replace them. So the economically active part of the population was becoming smaller and, increasingly, village communities were made up of older people who had only small incomes and therefore little to spend at their local store. It is true that the countryside has recently attracted new residents from urban areas, especially in commuter and retirement districts, but their numbers have been limited by strict control of housing development, and in any case many of the newcomers are car owners and prefer to do most of their shopping in larger centres.

The enormous rise in personal mobility is the second important factor. It is estimated that in 1938 there were under two million cars on the road, a figure which had grown to over fourteen million by the end of the 1970s. Cars have caused a revolution in people's shopping habits by opening up a choice of places to shop and enabling them to make fewer shopping trips. Younger men and women, in particular, choose to shop in towns because of the greater range and variety of goods and because it is more exciting. They may find the personal service in village shops offputting, and prefer the impersonality and convenience of the supermarket. People travelling to work, taking children to school, or going into a town for entertainment often use these trips for shopping as well. Those who do not own a car may rely on local bus or train services for transportation, although in some villages 'over sixties' clubs make special arrangements for such excursions. At Elmdon in Essex, for instance, the Evergreen Club takes its members in private cars once a week to Saffron Walden to shop and look around (although this has had the unwanted effect of reducing the local bus service still further). One result of the higher degree of car ownership in rural areas (caused partly by the decrease in public transport) has been to speed up the decline of rural transport services.

O.J. Birnage's shop, Charlbury, Oxfordshire.

Changes in retailing have also increased the attraction of urban shopping. Supermarkets have gained in popularity as they are usually accessible as well as offering cheap products. A single trip to the supermarket will enable a family to stock up with enough convenience foods to last a fortnight, and anyone with a home freezer (large sections of the population now own one) can store frozen foods for several months. The opening of hyper-markets and superstores on the edges of towns has strengthened the trend towards 'single stop' shopping. The last twenty-five years have seen a marked increase in multiple stores and a fall in the number of independent traders, especially grocers. In 1961 there were as many as 147,000 grocery outlets in the U.K. Now there are probably fewer than 39,000, with maybe no more than 9,000 in rural districts.

Since the abolition of Retail Price Maintenance in the early sixties, the village shopkeeper has been unable to compete in price with the giant multiples, such

Grocery and general store, Broadway, Worcestershire.

59

Farmers Weekly published this photograph on 25th March 1960, commenting of the changing times that 'even the village shop has its frozen food cabinet – with both British and foreign packs'. Note, however, that it was not yet thought necessary to keep the butter refrigerated!

Mr S. Coleman at work in his butcher's shop at Brookland, Kent, in July 1949. Note the butcher's block, over 150 years old, made of elm, four feet across. In 1931 the block cost Mr Coleman 7s 6d plus another 7s 6d to get it home.

as ASDA and Sainsburys. Often he cannot even buy goods wholesale at the prices at which supermarkets can afford to sell them retail. A few years ago, Derrick Roberts, a village shopkeeper in Bramshaw (in the New Forest), hit the headlines when he marched into his local Tesco supermarket with his fellow shopkeepers and bought up all the white bread, which was selling at a lower price than he was being charged by his suppliers. The big chains benefit from huge turnover, which enables them to bargain effectively with food manufacturers for the lowest possible prices, including the negotiation of special discount arrangements on such items as promotional packs, 'money-off' offers and competition goods. Village shopkeepers suffer twice from these so-called 'discriminatory discounts' – first, because their buying power does not allow them to demand similar reductions and second, because the manufacturer (who has to take his profits from somewhere) may well rely on the sales made to independent shopkeepers to help him give discounts to the larger customers. The multiples also gain because their costs of handling and distribution are lower (as goods are delivered in bulk to a relatively small number of stores) and labour costs are reduced by self-service within the store. Small rural shopkeepers cannot take advantage of these economies of scale and often find it difficult to obtain frequent deliveries of bread, cooked meats, frozen foods, etc., if their shop is not on a main traffic route. They are also more severely affected than their larger competitors by stock loss through the expiry of sell-by dates, particularly since recent problems with food contamination have highlighted the risks of breaking the cold chain. Some village shopkeepers say they never have anything fresh to eat – they live on outdated stock! Wages costs are kept down mainly by the use of family labour.

As well as the competition from the towns faced by village stores, other outlets such as mobile shops, farm shops and the petrol stations that sell food, confectionery and cigarettes pose a challenge.

Bill and Bess Godwin's store at Cambo, Northumberland.

The basic difficulty faced by the small village store is that of attracting loyal and regular customers. At present it is used chiefly by those local inhabitants who have no car or by the 'dammit' shoppers who have forgotten certain items in their regular weekly shop at a nearby supermarket. Non car owners (often the aged, the poor and the infirm) are frequently on a fairly strict budget, so their purchases are limited, and incidental or occasional shoppers, using the village store merely as a last resort, will buy only the odd item. Neither group is likely to provide the shopkeeper with an adequate income.

Crowcombe, Somerset, in 1984.

In fact many foodstore proprietors are able to hang on only by taking a smaller and smaller profit. Just after the war a well-run shop might expect as much as 20% net profit on turnover, whereas now, even a competently managed shop can make no more than 5% to 8%. As well as declining profitability, there is all too frequently a lack of working capital due to high repayments on loans, high rates and standing charges. Difficulties may also occur when a lease falls in and a new lease is obtainable only at a greatly increased rent. An enterprising shopkeeper may be penalised for his success if his landlord believes he can pay more, particularly if the shop is in a desirable location.

Some proprietors, of course, will be content if the shop just ticks over, deriving their satisfaction from being at the hub of village life and working at home. Indeed, some take up the occupation purely as a hobby, a retirement activity or because of a desire to 'get away from it all'. Hence Mr John Wood, a former engineer, took over the lease of a village shop at Simonburn near Hexham, County Durham, in 1984 simply because he likes 'the lifestyle of running a shop and post office in such an attractive village'. But he cheerfully admits that he would probably be better-off on the dole, since not more than £8 or £10 a day is going into the till: 'We have about half-a-dozen customers. From our last quarter's accounts, we are spending more than we are making. But I suppose a lot of people would pay to live here.'

This is an extreme example, but it is not unknown for those who do seek to earn a serious livelihood from their shop to find themselves subsidising it out of savings or another source of income. This has been the experience of Bill Godwin who, with his wife Bess, has looked after the village store in the picturesque but tiny village of Cambo in Northumberland since 1977. Previously, they had successfully run a shop in Newcastle with a turnover of between £2000 and £3000 a week, but they decided to move to the country when vandalism and crime in the neighbourhood became a worry. However, with under 300 souls

Pilsley Farm Shop, Chatsworth Estate, Derbyshire, in 1985.

and little passing trade, Cambo provided an insufficiency of custom, especially once economic recession had started to bite in the early 1980s. By 1984, turnover had fallen to a point where Bill Godwin was clearing only about £75 a week plus a small post-office salary. This meant that he was subsidising the shop to the tune of about £750 a year out of capital. Moreover, he could not simply close the shop, because as a self-employed person, he would receive no unemployment benefit, and in order to get any return on his private retirement schemes he had to keep going. It would have been impossible to make the necessary payments out of social security. In December 1986, Bill Godwin told me that the situation was no better, despite 'having tried everything and done our utmost to improve the shop'. He is now over sixty-five but has had to keep the shop open until the expiry of the lease in 1990. The property is owned by the National Trust and the accommodation is tied to the shop. Eventually the couple will have to move, but so far inflation has made it difficult for them to find an affordable cottage. If necessary, Bill Godwin will run down the grocery side of the business, just keeping on the sub post office. In the circumstances, he is understandably bitter as 'all I have worked for for years has gone down the drain'.

Other traders have directed their anger at local villagers. When Miss Hilda Shepherd shut up her family business for good in East Hanney (Oxfordshire) in March 1985 she commented:

'I am infuriated with those who say they will mourn the loss of the shops (another grocery store closed in neighbouring West Hanney at about the same time). If they really cared, they would have supported us.

'I could add up on one hand the number of pensioners who regularly shop here. You are lucky to get most in once in six months. I am grateful to those who regularly supported the business. But I am closing, and not selling as some people have suggested, because there just isn't enough trade.'

Sometimes, however, it is the action (or inaction) of the local authority which proves crucial to the survival of the village shopkeeper. Councils control or regulate many aspects of life which may make or break the fortunes of a village shop. For example, councils influence the number of potential customers through planning controls on land for new housing. Their planning powers also include regulating new retail outlets, controlling the appearance of properties and vetting applications for change of use, all of which can limit the freedom of the shopkeeeper to tailor his business to requirements. Even the extent to which councils permit external advertisements may draw or limit trade, as may their highways policy: the construction of bypasses usually diverts through traffic around villages (and therefore away from the shops) and the restriction of on-street parking may deter residents from stopping. In Upottery, Devon, a woman living in a cottage next to a pub applied to open a shop there in the knowledge that it had been a post office some thirty years before, but after a site visit the Planning Committee turned down the application on highway grounds. Despite assurances that barriers would be erected so that pedestrians did not cross the road outside the shop at a point judged to be dangerous, the road safety argument put forward by the County Surveyor prevailed and meant no shop for Upottery. Other policies pursued by county councils, such as the withdrawal of public transport services, may also have an adverse effect on village shops. In

Ian and Ann Baker's store at Dilton Marsh, near Trowbridge, Wiltshire, in 1983. The shop has been converted to self service, but the exterior had not yet been renovated when this photograph was taken.

some counties, the idea of 'key settlements' is pursued, this means that resources and amenities are concentrated in the larger villages, which often leads to a trade leakage to them away from businesses in the smaller ones. Planners are increasingly aware of the drawbacks of 'key settlement' policy, but schemes of this sort are still being put into practice.

Nonetheless, much continues to depend on the personality and enterprise of the individual shopkeeper. A welcoming smile and a cheerful, efficient manner are still valuable assets. So, too, is a determination to succeed. Providing the shop is made clean and attractive with an adequate range of goods and strict financial control over every aspect of the undertaking, it will still have a reasonable chance of success. But the day of the worst sort of village shop, with its musty interior, dead flies in the window, and miscellaneous assortment of often unknown and overpriced stock is over – or at least nearly over!

Some of the ingredients of success can be identified in the experience of Ian and Ann Baker at their village store at Dilton Marsh near Westbury in Wiltshire. Their first priority before taking over the shop in 1982 was to make sure that they had chosen a site with enough potential customers. They converted the premises to a self-service store and installed new lighting and a food freezer to provide a clean, hygienic and convenient selling area. Ian's approach was to move up-market by developing a range of quality goods for which customers would be prepared to pay a premium. He commented: 'A tin of Heinz beans, a jar of Nescafé or even a packet of Dairylea is the same wherever you buy it, only

Hurst Stores, Berkshire, 1989.

the price can differ. But with good groceries price tends to be largely unimport-
ant'. Profit areas soon included such special lines as fresh fruit and vegetables,
cooked meats and delicatessen foods, and wines and spirits. In order to obtain
a better deal on basic stock they joined the MACE symbol group and also obtained some goods from a local cash and carry. Brand leaders as well as MACE's
own label products were stocked, a combination which worked well. Deliveries

were undertaken and the local inhabitants kept informed of special promotions by means of leaflets. Stock management was strict and constantly monitored. Within a few months of the new shop starting to trade, sales had risen by 30% and gross profits had grown to 20%. Since then Ian and Ann Baker have moved to a larger MACE store 'with three times the area and twice the turnover' in Weston-super-Mare, Somerset.

Not all 'go-ahead' owners convert to self-service. Some, like Richard Booth trading in the village of Sleights in the Whitby area of Yorkshire, emphasise traditional features:

'I don't want to be a mini-supermarket. I have styled the fascia with a period image in mind and I want to keep it that way. There is some self-service with a few baskets by the door. But it is mostly counter-trade'.

He and his wife Lynda insist instead on quality and service, making no attempt to compete directly in price with nearby urban supermarkets. The needs of pensioners are catered for by stocking plenty of lines in small sizes 'which go

Bob and Pat Dawes' Food and Wine Shop at High Halden, near Ashford, Kent.

very well', but most of the expansion in the shop's business has come from non-food lines and particularly from newspapers:

'If you want to survive in a village you must either have news or a post office. There was already a post office in Sleights so newspapers were an obvious area to concentrate on.'

The shop is also distinctive in so far as it is 'computerised', although as a means of accounting, Richard Booth feels that the micro is a useful though not essential gadget.

Developing a range of specialised 'value added' goods often pays dividends. A very few shops such as Pat Rance's cheese emporium at Streatley, Berkshire, can gain almost a national reputation, while others draw custom from a wide local catchment area. For instance, one enthusiastic customer describes Mr and Mrs Arnold's Buckland Stores at Betchworth, Surrey, as 'the most idyllic store – with a range of foods to put Harrod's Food Hall to shame'. No doubt there is a little poetic licence in this statement, but the same determination to diversify can be seen in this report of Sally and Hilaire Pugh's shop at Marton in Shropshire:

'The range of goods is extensive from meat, bread and cakes, delicatessen with a variety of cheeses to general provisions, confectionery and toiletries. Papers and bread are delivered daily and fresh fruit and vegetables are of a good standard. The shop has a licence for the sale of alcohol and table wines purchased there have been commended by experts . . . The Pughs make every effort to keep up with modern trends, stocking high-fibre-content lines, vegetarian foods and prepared dishes, and do test runs on items such as pure fruit jams, unsweetened tinned fruits and so on.'

Some shops have even found a growing demand for 'real bread' following the campaigns for 'real ale' and 'real cheese'. Catering for minority tastes, however, is not without its dangers, and higher priced quality foods may not sell well in depressed areas, as Bill Godwin had learnt to his cost in Northumberland by 1984:

'Somebody asked for stuffed chicken roll. I bought it, but only sold half and half had to be thrown away. At one time we had ten different delicatessen meats, now we have three because we can't afford the wastage. We had such a range of epicure foods we were known as the mini-Fortnums.'

Two years later he had given up fresh bacon and fresh meat altogether, as these had become entirely uneconomic.

Another means of trying to ensure the viability of a shop is by adding on services on an agency basis. The most important of these is running a sub post office and the income supplement received for this keeps many small country businesses afloat. Remuneration increases with the work done but is on a scale that guarantees that smaller offices earn proportionately more than larger ones. Those offices with a total traffic of below 21,600 units a year are paid a minimum figure, presently about £2,300, and there is also a pro-rata scale for new part-time offices. The importance of a sub post office, though, is that its services draw people into the shop so that they are tempted into making additional purchases. The same is true of selling newspapers. Other useful agencies include

Richard and Lynda Booth's shop at Sleights,
Yorkshire.

Opposite. Top left: The Epicure Ham Co. Ltd, Upton-on-Severn, Worcestershire. *Top right:* The sub post office at Combe, Oxfordshire. *Below:* Michael and Marian's Post Office Stores and Newsagents, Tingewick, Buckinghamshire.

Major Pat Rance in the cheese cellar of the family shop at Streatley, Berkshire, which arguably stocks the most interesting selection of cheeses to be found in Britain.

A newsagent and tobacconist's at Castleton in the Derbyshire Peak District. This 1930s scene shows the influence of developing tourism.

dry cleaning, shoe repairs, film processing, video films, Interflora, wines and spirits and coach bookings.

In holiday areas shops may try to sell craft products or other items catering to the tripper or tourist trade. At Newdigate village stores in Surrey, Mr and Mrs Calcutt have opened a coffee shop and encourage local craftsmen and artists to display their work there. On show are locally produced embroidery, soft toys, knitwear, silk flowers, tapestry and paintings, all of which can be purchased or commissioned. Special events are organised to show how to make pottery or press flowers. This is on top of normal retailing activities, of which John Calcutt notes, 'we are constantly on the lookout for new product lines so that our range is as complete as possible'. He adds, 'The shop is moderately supported by local people, but most of the trade in the coffee shop comes from people out for a drive in the country who happen to see our sign'.

Similarly, Mr and Mrs Hanlon have succeeded in building up a goodish passing trade at their Minions Post Office stores near Liskeard in Cornwall. Despite its bleak setting – it is reputedly the highest shop in Cornwall, with no ready clientele – it attracts tourists who have come to see the 'Cheesewring', a natural granite rock formation on the south eastern edge of Bodmin Moor. Shops do well in other holiday locations if they are near a caravan site, camping ground or self-catering apartments. There is also the possibility that shops such as these can act as agents for the local tourist board. Indeed, this is already happening in parts of Northumberland and will soon happen in the Peak District, on the basis that an honorarium of £100 a year is paid in return for the stocking and distribution of tourist leaflets.

Another tried formula is to 'open all hours', especially in areas where it is possible to catch people passing to and from work. Evening opening will make sense if there is an off licence, and Sunday mornings can be profitable where newspapers are sold. Long working hours, however, can take their toll, and the strain on a marriage can be considerable, not least when there is a mountain of

Groups of independent wholesalers provide village shopkeepers with some of the advantages of bulk-buying. Here, Mr Brian Hutchinson, a member of the MACE group, is seen outside his shop at Easingwold, Yorkshire, in 1986.

paperwork to be tackled in the evenings after closing time. Yet proper profit and loss accounting, making regular VAT and income tax returns, and careful stock-taking are all essential to a sound business. The size of turnover alone is no guarantee of profitability, as the new owners of the East Mersea village shop in Essex, which opened in 1983, discovered: 'Despite £34,000 going into the tills, to our surprise our accountant produced a loss for the first half year'. Their outgoings had by far exceeded expectations, and in particular the electricity bill was huge.

There are, of course, ways in which village shopkeepers can make worthwhile economies, as a report by the Building Design Partnership points out: 'They can reduce overheads by, for instance, applying for rates relief, using economy meters for electricity supply and insulating fridges, and even claiming tax relief on the cost of the canine pet/security guard'.

The village stores at Newdigate, Surrey. *Opposite:* The post office and stores, Abbots Ann, Hampshire, 1988.

In addition, proprietors can buy their stock more cheaply by joining one of the voluntary wholesaling groups, such as MACE, SPAR, VG, etc., which try to extend the advantages of bulk buying to independent grocers. Even so, some groups are reluctant to service the small, remote village store and impose a sliding scale of charges which benefits the larger urban independents. At the same time they are anxious to increase their sales of low-margin products, for instance, by deep-cut price promotions, which may mean, in the words of one rural retailer, 'small dividends and almost zero profits'. The main alternative source of supply is the wholesale cash-and-carry, although a village shopkeeper may find it difficult to leave his premises to obtain goods, or may find that the cash-and-carry is out of stock of the items he requires when he gets there. Physical strength should also be take into consideration, since everything has to be lifted four times between the cash-and-carry and the shop and so one ton of goods becomes four tons by the time it is on the shop shelf. Another problem is that the cash-and-carry tends to deal in large pack sizes, which are unsuitable for many rural customers' needs and tie up the shopkeeper's capital for too long. Again, he or she may face the ludicrous situation that the nearest supermarket is the cheapest and most convenient supplier.

Considering the number of pitfalls, it is scarcely surprising that many shops go under. The survival rate for new entrants into the occupation is low. In some areas of the country, not more than fifty per cent are likely to get through the first two or three years. Under-capitalisation and a heavy mortgage are among the chief causes of failure. In this respect Ian and Ann Baker at Dilton Marsh in Wiltshire were exceptional as, in their early thirties, they were able to buy their shop outright as well as having the benefit of a fair degree of financial underpinning. They also had family contacts in the grocery trade – a background which proved helpful in their bid to join the MACE symbol group, since MACE would not usually have considered such a small outlet. The Bakers' successor at the Dilton Marsh store inherited the advantage of a 'built-up' business, but faced stiff competition from a new Tesco on the outskirts of Trowbridge, which runs free buses to the surrounding villages. This so-called 'courtesy service' is a growing threat in many areas of the country. Mr and Mrs Calcutt at Newdigate are confronting the same problem. The opening of a Tesco superstore at Gatwick in March 1986 – with free transportation laid on – led to an immediate 20% drop in the Calcutt's takings, which has now levelled off at 10%. The enterprising owners are presently racking their brains as to how to turn their old bakehouse into a profitable new sideline!

Few rural shopkeepers can afford to be complacent even if their own business is well-founded. The disappearance of a neighbouring retailer will have serious consequences if it leads to trade disappearing from the village. This has often been the case where a number of specialist retailers (ironmonger, chemist, greengrocer and butcher, etc.) have between them provided an almost complete range of services to the local community. When one goes, the rest tend sooner or later to follow. Awareness of this mutual dependence was clear recently in the Oxfordshire village of Goring-on-Thames, where the closing of the launderette in a small arcade of shops caused other traders to fear that their summer trade would be affected, as a result of those holidaying on the river choosing to stop at Pangbourne or Wallingford instead.

The closure of a sub post office is frequently a sign of terminal decline. This may occur on the retirement or resignation of the sub post master. It is rarely the result of deliberate Post Office policy, although the decision to encourage the payment of pensions and other automated benefits into bank accounts has not helped, as it reduces the need to use the post office facility. If the retiring sub post master owns the building and wishes to convert the business area into domestic living space, it may well be impossible to recruit someone willing to risk starting up at a new location, and once a sub post office has closed, villagers may find they have to travel several miles for their small postal necessities, DHSS payments or National Girobank transactions.

On the positive side it can be said that since 1984 the Post Office has shown a greater commitment to maintaining rural services by agreeing to allow certain sub post offices to open part-time, particularly where the option of a part-time contract makes it easier to fill vacancies. However, in July 1987 the Post Office dropped a real bombshell, by decreeing that all offices below 50,000 units would, when they next change hands, be designated 'community' post offices, in other words they would become *compulsory* part-time offices. The district managers will decide for how many hours each of the 4,500 offices in question (all in rural areas) will open, but in many cases it will be fewer than ten hours per week, and annual salaries for staff will often drop to about £1000 per annum.

Sub postmasters are strongly resisting these changes, introduced as a means of saving money for the Post Office. Unfortunately, they were agreed with Post Office (Counters) Ltd. by their union, the National Federation of Sub-Postmasters. The main grounds of complaint are that the value of their businesses has been badly affected, that the remuneration is totally inadequate for the work involved, and the fact that it is difficult to explain to someone coming in with a parcel that the shop is open but the post office is closed.

The last has not been heard of this problem, as many MPs, councillors, rural community councils and other organisations are determined to do battle on what is seen as a further attack on rural amenities. The survival of the sub post office-cum-food-shop-cum newsagents – is crucial since its closure when it is the last shop in the village, can have a devastating effect on the old, the sick and the disabled. What is lost is not only the shop itself but a meeting point and a life-line in time of need. As Caroline Walker puts it, 'Will Tesco's bring your pension? Will Sainsbury's open their door after 8pm to get you a sticking plaster?' The best village shopkeeper is also a good friend and confidant, who will perform a host of small personal services for the customers, as a result of an intimate knowledge of their needs and circumstances, as well as contributing time and labour selflessly to the community as a whole. This sense of caring and of social responsibility is evident, for instance, in the shop run by Mrs Beeb at Hadnall in Shropshire:

'Myself, and five part-time assistants, all local women, serve the customers with everything, from fresh bread and milk, to paraffin and chicken corn. If we can't sell them that we'll try and sell them raffle tickets, dance and disco, and cheese and wine tickets. All these functions are held to raise funds for the old folk, church and of course the village hall. The villagers all tend to think we know everything that's going on in the village and that we are very nosy, but this isn't the case, everyone comes in and tells us all the good and bad news, we hear the

Derek and Val Vine's '8 till late' Spar store at Sothcott's, Bembridge, Isle of Wight.

Opposite. Top left: The Pharmacy, Charlbury, Oxfordshire. *Top right:* Shoe shop, Dulverton, Somerset. *Centre left:* Thame, Oxfordshire. *Centre right:* Butcher's and poulterer's, Godstone, Surrey. *Bottom left:* Gentlemen's hairdresser and *bottom right* butcher's shop at Lostwithiel, Cornwall. All photographed in 1976.

complaints and praises of anything in the village, some things we'd rather not hear. If anyone requires a plumber, sweep, electrician or part-time job it is all on the notice board in the shop window. They can pick up their other fresh foods, such as vegetables, prescriptions left by the chemist or doctor from Clive in the shop, also their football coupons which they return by Friday for the agents to collect. Any spare Hadnall newsletters and church newsletters are always on the counter for anyone to pick up, also on a Thursday the Admag is available. We also have left in the shop the leisure classes leaflet from Shrewsbury and Shawbury. These are very popular, but whether anyone attends the classes is another matter.

'At the moment we are organising the village fete, which is being held in July, again I have offered the services of the shop as a dropping off point for items for the tombola stall and the white elephant stall. I am sure we'll not be able to move in our hallway soon for bags and boxes, this also applies when a rummage sale is coming up . . .

'We do seven delivery rounds a week in a caravan, taking orders as far as Cold Hatton and Ellerdine (ten miles away), and Baschurch (nine miles away) in the opposite direction. On the van we take out prescriptions and as many old folk

The Ellesmere Centre, Stetchworth, Cambridgeshire.

live a few miles from their local post office, or have lost it, so they have transferred their books to my office which I put up for them so they have no worries about getting their money regularly every week. There is some threat to rural offices, being closed in the near future I believe, so we just hope and pray we are left in safety. If I lost my office I am afraid a lot of jobs would be lost as well'.

One way of maintaining some of the services formerly provided by a village shop after it has closed (when there is no likelihood that it will be reopened as a commercial enterprise), is to set up a community shop. Among the better known ventures are Shillingford and Letcombe Basset in Oxfordshire, Tivetshall St Mary in Norfolk, Debden in Essex, the Brentor Community Centre in Devon; and the Ellesmere Centre at Stetchworth, Cambridgeshire. In 1979 Letcombe was faced with a crisis: the couple who had run the Post Office Store had to give up as a result of ill-health and it was clear that in this small village of 165 no one would be able to make a go of a new business. So it was decided to try to establish a community shop. The organisers were fortunate in being able to build on the experience of the nearby village of Shillingford, which had successfully run a shop since 1974. The Vale of the White Horse District Council agreed to rent premises to local people providing they kept costs down by erecting the prefabricated building themselves. Secondhand fittings and equipment were donated by the Oxford and Swindon Cooperative, who gave advice on how to manage the shop and supplied goods on favourable terms enabling them to be sold at normal Coop prices. More recently, since the closure of the Wantage branch, however, most groceries have been obtained from Mr Bull, an independent retailer at Grove.

80

Other fresh foods, such as vegetables, are purchased from a local mobile, at a 10% to 15% discount, and meat is supplied by the Danish Bacon company. The stock level is held steady at a value of about £830, which is equivalent to three weeks' takings. One of the principal organisers, Mrs Wilde, notes that the trick is 'not to try to do too much or to hold stock for too long'. The average profit margin is approximately 8%. Most villagers use the shop because it is handy for topping up purchases they have made elsewhere, but a few use it for their basic shopping. It is staffed by volunteers and managed by a committee which meets three times a year. It opens for between one and four hours every day of the week and has kept going successfully (with minor ups and downs) for the last six and a half years. Apart from its evident usefulness as a shop, it is valued as a social amenity.

The establishment in 1981 of a community store at Debden (population 750) also followed the loss of its only shop in 1976. A public meeting was held to see

The Ellesmere Centre, Stetchworth, Cambridgeshire.

Debden Community Shop, Essex.

whether there was sufficient support for a community shop and an encouraging response led to the formation of a committee of eight. The entire village was canvassed to identify those prepared to offer practical help and to sell 'grocery vouchers' which would provide some initial finance, and could be exchanged for goods when the shop opened. Nearly £600 was raised and promises of help were received from over 40 people. An old mobile home was converted to provide premises and the parish council gave permission for it to be sited on the edge of the recreation ground as well as offering a loan of £200 towards the cost of equipment. At first there were 18 volunteers to staff the shop, some willing to work one two-hour session each week, others one session a fortnight. Other volunteers took responsibility for ordering, pricing, stocking the shelves and cleaning. By 1983, the shop had become successful enough to warrant new premises, and in November 1983 an extension was opened with the necessary

Promotional material put out by COSIRA (now the Rural Development Commission), the Rural Community Councils and National Girobank.

capital coming from Essex County Council, local fund-raising and a small bank loan. The shop now incorporates a sub post office run not by the group but by an individual who pays a rental for the space. The range of goods carried by the shop covers all basic needs including fresh fruit, vegetables and frozen meat, plus a number of sideline items designed to attract people into the shop. Goods are bought from two cash-and-carry outlets or, in the case of some fresh foods, are delivered. Prices on known value products (standard items whose value is generally known to the public) are kept on a par with those at the local cooperative store, usually producing only a 2% or 3% profit margin, although luxury items may be marked up as much as 40%. In 1983 the shop had an average weekly turnover of £600 with a maximum of £1,200 giving a gross profit of about £5,000 or 15.9%. A satisfactory level of profitability has been maintained by a simple but efficient system of stock control, aided by regular advertising in leaflets and monthly newsletters which remind inhabitants that the shop is there to be used. The surplus has been used to extend the stock range, buy new equipment and to pay a modest wage on hours worked over and above two per month. So Debden has created a new type of village shop which flourishes on a combination of community service and sound commercial principles.

Another type of experiment is the Ellesmere Centre – a multipurpose extension to the village hall at Stetchworth in Cambridgeshire. This has been financed by the Development Commission, the local authority and the Sports Council and provides sports, social and welfare facilities as well as a community shop. One of the most significant aspects of the Centre was the appointment of a Community Officer to develop its various functions and to expand the commercial activities of the shop which opened in 1984. It was the only one in the village and despite some difficulties has proved to be very popular, especially with the elderly. The project was grant-aided until 1987 by Cambridgeshire County Council and can be seen as a precedent for local authority involvement of a similar kind in other parts of the country.

The community shop, though, is not a universal solution. Its success depends largely on the efforts of volunteers and it will last only as long as their enthusiasm remains. After four or five years the constant commitment for little or no financial reward can become tedious, and disenchantment may set in. At this point, unless new blood is introduced, the venture may falter, as was the case with the Shillingford Community Shop, which closed early in 1986.

A far more acceptable long-term solution is to sustain independent shopkeepers wherever possible. Help is available from a number of sources, including the Rural Community Councils of England and Wales. These are county-based voluntary organisations whose aim it is to promote the social and economic well-being of the countryside. They generally consist of various social, welfare and environmental organisations within the relevant county, with a small permanent staff, and are funded by the Rural Development Commission, local government and voluntary sources. From the mid-'seventies, Countryside Officers were appointed with a stronger brief to carry the work of the RCCs into the villages and to appraise their particular needs, and a number of reports were produced highlighting the decline of rural services. These results tallied with those of a number of other surveys carried out at the same time, originating principally from the University of East Anglia and St David's University

College, Lampeter. In May 1982 a meeting, jointly organised by the National Council for Voluntary Organisations and the Development Commission, was held at Gloucester and attended by representatives from over 70 interested bodies. Out of this came a publication *Support for Village Shops* which aimed to identify the action that could be taken to assist country shopkeepers by central and local government, the retail industries and voluntary organisations.

One positive result of this growing pressure was the Government's decision in March 1983 to widen the responsibilities of COSIRA (the Council for Small Industries in Rural Areas) to include the needs of country retailers and the advisory duties previously carried out by the Community Councils. Until this point, COSIRA's role had been limited to rural manufacturing and service industries. This new initiative meant that a full-time retail officer was appointed, whose job it was to publicise the difficulties faced by rural shopkeepers, to lobby on their behalf, and to direct the work of five (now nine) regional consultants. The first retail officer, John White, was formerly a Hereford shopkeeper, while his successor, David Lingham, has worked in the bakery, grocery and hardware trades – an excellent background for an understanding of the problems involved in rural trading. Consultants were also chosen for their experience in retailing and running training programmes as well as for the range of skills they could provide within the group. They were not strictly speaking COSIRA staff, but were employed as required to a budget maximum of 176 days a year. The main priority was to provide help and advice to general stores and sub post offices under threat of closure in single shop villages, particularly in areas designated as Special Development Areas.

In April 1988, the Development Commission and its main agency, COSIRA, merged to form the Rural Development Commission. The aim of this new body is to give effective promotion to jobs and businesses in the countryside, concentrating on the twenty-eight newly designated Rural Development Areas, which are chiefly located in the north and east of England, the border counties and the south-west. The role of the specialist retail adviser and his team of consultants has not changed. The counselling service to village shopkeepers is based on at least one entirely confidential visit to the shop, as a result of which suggestions will be made as to how maximum profitability can be gleaned from the business. Advice includes stocking policies, stock turnover, wholesale purchasing, merchandising, etc., as well as the more generalised guidance on business management available to all rurally based firms. The Commission also runs a series of seminars entitled 'Buying a Village Shop', as research has shown that many shops are ill-managed because their owners are largely ignorant of the trade they have taken on. Other short training courses are provided by independent companies such as Retail Advisory Services of Hereford as well as by voluntary wholesale groups for their members. A series of four training films sponsored by Nurdin & Peacock Ltd (cash and carry wholesalers) have been produced, focusing on the 'Little Shop of Horrors' and starring Rodney Bewes, Nerys Hughes and Kenneth Williams. These show how not to run a small shop and then how to run one successfully. The difference the right advice can make is amply illustrated by the experience of Dreena and Patrick Hanlan, who decided to change direction and become village shopkeepers: 'My husband was approaching 40 and realised he didn't know what to do with his life. He had a very good

Steeple Aston Post Office and Stores, Wiltshire, 1989.

job as a banker and commuted to London from our Sussex home and he was fed up with the two hour journey each way!'

Their first move was to contact the Sussex branch of the Rural Development Commission, who sent around 'a nice man who ran his own supermarket, so he was well-qualified to discuss our needs. He went through every angle with us from financing a shop to the area in which to set up in!'

The Hanlans decided on Cornwall – a place they'd always liked, and were then put in touch with the Commission's Cornwall Representative, who advised on which villages to investigate. When they had found a property which seemed to fill the bill, the Rural Development Commission vetted it, showed the couple how to estimate the shop's profitability before purchase (including the post office side of the business), and helped with evaluation of the shop's accounts for the last three years. They even suggested where to go for a mortgage.

Since then – five years ago – the Minion Stores has prospered and the family is happy with its new lifestyle: 'The children have a marvellous time and we've made some good friends', commented Mrs. Hanlan in 1987. 'The business is going extremely well. We've only paid £12.00 for all Rural Development's help because we only had one formal session. The rest of the advice came by phone and they didn't charge for that'.

Village shops can usually benefit from more publicity. In the early 1980s many of the Rural Community Councils launched their own campaigns under slogans like 'Be Parochial Shop Local' and 'Use it or Lose it'. The aim was to make the local population more aware of the importance of village shops and to point out how essential it is that people use them. Comparisons were made between prices in a village shop and those in a neighbouring supermarket, taking into account the cost of using a private car to shop outside the village. Information from these 'shopping basket surveys' was then publicised through posters, hand-outs, the local papers and radio stations. The results showed that although prices in village shops were frequently higher than in supermarkets, the margin could be extremely narrow once transport was taken into consideration.

Ivinghoe Post Office and Stores, Buckinghamshire, 1989.

Local media attention can also be attracted through Best Village Shopkeeper competitions, again organised by the RCCs. Probably the first of these was held in North Shropshire in 1981 and since then the idea has been imitated in most English counties. In Cambridgeshire, for example, the 1986 Village Shop of the Year Award (for villages with only one shop) was won by the Brinkley Post Office Stores run by Mrs J.E. Fane who received a plaque and a cheque for £30 presented by COSIRA. For villages with more than one shop, the award went to Mr and Mrs Reinemann of Haslingfield Post Office.

One of the most important developments over the last few years has been the formation of Village Shopkeepers Associations, stimulated by COSIRA and the RCCs. Despite some early hesitancy on the part of shopkeepers, the movement has grown rapidly since its inception. The first VSA was formed in Hampshire in February 1984 under the chairmanship of John Sheppard. It is still probably the largest association, although there are now some 43 in existence, covering most parts of the country and with over 2000 members. What happened in Somerset is fairly typical. A shopkeeper approached the RCC and with the aid of COSIRA a meeting was set up in a local pub which was publicised through an announcement in the local press and personal telephone calls. A total of 23 people attended the meeting and unanimously agreed to form an Association. The first year's subscription of £10 was also agreed and paid on the night, with the COSIRA retail officer acting as an interim treasurer until office bearers were elected. The aims of the West Somerset Association of Village Shopkeepers are to provide a forum at which examples of good practice can be shared and ways of improving trade discussed as well as to give members a representative voice for collective action on issues which affect them. In particular, the Association hopes to present the views and interests of village shopkeepers more forcefully to local planning authorities, other relevant officials, community leaders and MPs. The general picture of the associations has been one of mixed success. Cornwall has over 200 members, and many others are thriving – notably in Oxfordshire, South Cumbria and Lancashire. Some, however, have fallen by the wayside as the original enthusiasts have left the trade and it has proved difficult to replace them.

One obvious way in which government could help is by providing direct financial aid. To date, the only grant aid has been by three English county councils under their Small Businesses Grant Schemes. Northumberland County Council and Cleveland County Council inaugurated these in 1978, followed by Shropshire County Council in 1980. The two earlier schemes, however, have now both excluded village shops from eligibility on the grounds that the service sector was the most risky to support and that money could be better spent on creating new jobs in other occupations. Shropshire alone is persisting with its programme, in which grants of up to £2000 may be made to assist in the purchase or adaptation of premises or internal fittings. Even so, few applications have been received (due partly to scant publicity) and a mere handful of individuals have benefited. More could be done.

Norway has possibly set an example for a national approach. In 1976, following the recommendation of a Royal Commission, the Norwegian government launched a programme of aid to help save village shops in sparsely populated areas. This took the form of grants for shop modernisation and expansion, income supplements for businesses with insufficient potential customers and grants for the development of a training and consultancy system. The aims have been to promote both business efficiency and customer loyalty in rural areas. According to Dr David Kirby, the scheme has been useful although the need for aid has proved permanent. The chief problem with implementing such a scheme in Britain would be its cost, although it might be that E.E.C. funds could be tapped to help the more disadvantaged areas.

There is no reason, of course, why other bodies should not be involved in offering financial assistance to shopkeepers. It has often been said that banks and the retail industry might show a greater degree of flexibility and support, but their contribution will, of course, always be limited as their commercial interests lie in the business of making money rather than distributing it. There could, perhaps, be further increases in the agency fee paid by the Post Office to sub post masters. The Post Office and the National Girobank have already made a substantial gesture in one respect: in October 1982, they jointly instigated a £3½ million scheme allowing sub post masters to borrow up to £10,000 from the National Girobank at a low rate of interest, repayable over three to five years, for the improvement of their business facilities, as well as overall modification of premises. These loans, however, are obviously of benefit only to stores which are already economically viable and where there is some hope of being able to repay them.

Now that the arrangements for the National Girobank to be sold off have been finalised, its relationship to the village shop may become much more problematical, although one might make the point that a buyer who decided not to work through the sub post office network would have to find 22,000 new outlets – a daunting prospect.

Other measures which would be welcomed by village shopkeepers would be the simplification of VAT, tax relief, or the reduction of rates on commercial premises. The annual rates bill is usually a substantial burden, and under the existing local rating system there are considerable differences – and anomalies – between rating authorities. Its scrapping and the introduction of a unified business rate in 1990 seemed to present a golden opportunity for reform, but initial indications (at the time of going to press) seem to suggest that although some shopkeepers will benefit, many will bear an even heavier burden than before. Once again, the precarious existence of small shopkeepers in general seems not to have been taken properly into account.

A reform that would be a good deal more popular with small shopkeepers (but is highly unlikely) would be the introduction of legislation to end discriminatory discounting by manufacturers or distributors, which at present gives the large store multiples enormous price advantages. But banning the practice would inevitably lead to a rise in the price of food and have an inflationary effect on the cost of living. So no government could contemplate this form of action.

An entirely different solution would be to pay rural retailers for providing certain welfare services. This would acknowledge the social as well as the economic role of the village shopkeeper, and give shape and substance to the range of activities frequently undertaken voluntarily out of a sense of local responsibility. John White, in urging this view, has suggested that the new 'community caretakers' might serve as outposts of the Citizens Advice Bureaux, if only in the

Opposite: Mrs Cox's General Stores, Woodcote, Oxfordshire, 1976.

Wookey Post Office Stores, Somerset, in 1985. The proprietor is being visited by retail consultant Peter Binden from the Rural Development Commission.

sense of assisting with simple form-filling and advising people where to get which kind of help. They might also deliver prescriptions and library books to housebound people, and perhaps organise a village taxi/bus service. They might even be involved in operating a lifeline call system for the aged. They would be paid on an agency basis for each service performed. A plan of this sort could actually make economic sense if it offered savings on services which are at present run by different organisations at a high cost and with low efficiency. For the future, modern computer technology offers the possibility (for those so-minded) of developing the role of a local information station and nerve-centre for the village community as a whole. One advantage of this kind of scheme is that it overcomes the taint of charity attached to the receiving of direct aid, which many shopkeepers find repugnant. It would also be proof against the objection that it

discriminated against small corner shops in urban areas (which also have a social role to play) since remuneration would be tied strictly to work done.

There are, of course, obvious difficulties. There is the matter of whether village shopkeepers would welcome such a new career and whether they would adapt easily to it. This would depend partly on the training provided, since certain professional skills would have to be acquired. Clearly too, habits of discretion would have to be cultivated, as a 'gossipy' image would destroy any confidence the public might have in such a development. Initially, only a few villages in a county might wish to take part in any pilot scheme, but eventually the problem of selection would have to be confronted. In villages with more than one shop, on what basis would government contracts be awarded? It might indeed be difficult to make a fair and impartial choice, especially where the decision might result in the loser going out of business.

The welfare option is a valuable one, but most shopkeepers will doubtless continue to see themselves first and foremost as traders, who will take their chance in the marketplace. What then, are their prospects in the run-up to the year 2000? Are they, as one commentator puts it, 'simply on a hiding to nothing'? So far, over the last half century, the story has certainly been one of increasing difficulties and decline, yet the picture is not one of unrelieved gloom.

There have been and still are successful village entrepreneurs who 'can always make a living if not a fortune' and who view the next decade or so with modest optimism. This is particularly true in predominantly middle-class localities, in the affluent residential areas of the larger cities and in retirement and seaside areas. Some villages in these regions have actually gained shops and a new pattern of shopping has emerged. The old-fashioned type of village store or even specialist retailer has given way to the dealer in antiques or china and jewellery, while a small-scale arcade development may house a delicatessen, ladies' hairdresser or flower and garden shop. There may also be a branch of a local firm of estate agents and perhaps an off licence or outpost of the Victoria Wine empire. The village pub will often have been turned into a licensed restaurant catering for the whole family, with an 'adventure' playground for children. In such high-income zones, the growth of superstores and hypermarkets in out-of-town sites may not necessarily have a disastrous effect on the village shop. It is more likely to be the small-town supermarket which is squeezed out, leaving the village shopkeeper specialising in high-quality, value-added products, which complement rather than compete with purchases from the price-conscious multiples. So the outlook may not be too unpromising for enterprising shopkeepers in areas of growing rural population, especially where residents have arrived as a result of outmigration from the suburbs.

But even in the richer pastures of southern England and perhaps East Anglia, now reportedly so full of 'Eastern promise', a proportion of shops will fail. This is particularly true of food shops, as the size of population required to support a shop rises all the time. (It was cheering to note, however, the attention paid by Anglia TV, local radio, and newspapers to the doubling in size of Tony and Sandra Gleed's shop at Tendring, in Essex. Several years before they had asked for advice from COSIRA's retail adviser, and had carried out all his suggestions plus many ideas of their own, with the result that sales had gone up ten-fold. However, perhaps the fact that the story was so very newsworthy indicates just how rarely this happens!) Research carried out by Norfolk County Council's planning department suggests that while in 1950 a population of about 400 was required to sustain a food store, by 1980 the corresponding figure was 800. This trend is illustrated in Dorset where the 1984 Village Facilities Survey, carried out by the County Council, revealed that since 1979 fourteen villages had lost a food shop, while a further fourteen had lost the only food shop they had. It is unlikely that these will re-open, unless it is with a change of use. Equally serious in Dorset's case was the fact that thirteen villages had lost their post offices in the previous five years, of which nine were full-time offices and four part-time. What was especially worrying was the fact that the rate of loss seemed to be greater than in the previous survey period. Only the number of specialist shops catering specifically to visitors (such as craft and souvenir shops) had increased. Since then the situation has continued to deteriorate, as David Fox, Dorset Community Council's Field Officer, informed me in a communication dated November 1986:

'Suffice it to say that since the publication of the report some 12 villages have lost their Post Office, and of these 5 were also shops. In one instance I was able to help with the retention of the postal counter facilities in alternative private premises, but the shop facility was irretrievably lost.'

The outlook for every type of shop in more remote localities in the north of the country and in non-tourist locations in Wales is blacker. Here, in areas of falling population and rising unemployment, the number of shops and other rural amenities will continue to fall sharply unless there is a change in Government policy. The Cleveland Rural Voice Committee, for instance, initiated a survey which reported in 1985 that 40% to 47% of existing village shops in Cleveland could be at risk.

In terms of the national picture, the 1986 report by the Building Design Partnership suggests that out of every ten businesses no more than three will be commercially sound and 'above concern' while one is likely to be in dire circumstances to which there is no long-term solution. The remaining six will be in a state of flux, either preceeding or following a change in ownership, and so will have an uncertain future.

The work being undertaken by the RCCs and The Rural Development Commission with regard to village shops is of undeniable importance and provides useful assistance. But further state aid is necessary, as is more local authority intervention, perhaps along the lines indicated. In addition, there is a strong case for amending planning restrictions to allow moderate housing and economic development in parishes in the more disadvantaged regions. This might involve a revision of county structure plans and would call for positive rather than merely passive policies towards retail provision, by giving retailers the same type of help afforded to industry. It might also require a more determined shift away from key settlement planning – assisting only the centres of population on a hierarchical basis – to a type of planning that would ensure that services and resources go to where they are most needed irrespective of the size of settlement.

Village shops are today at a crossroads in their history. It is now vital that village shopkeepers should themselves express an opinion as to how they see the future and should press for those practical resources needed to allow them to realise it.

Appendices

The Ellesmere Centre Community Co-operative

The shop was opened in May 1984 in the Ellesmere Centre in Stetchworth. Five individuals loaned £300 each for stock. This amount was repaid in two instalments during the second year of trading. A Community Co-ordinator was appointed for the day-to-day running of the Ellesmere Centre, and 50% of her time was spent in the day-to-day running of the shop. She did not commence until July 1984 so Mrs Bendon was responsible for the first two months. It was felt that as the shop would be staffed mainly by volunteers, each working a three-hour shift (either morning or afternoon), it was necessary to have one person to provide continuity – for ordering stock, helping volunteers in the beginning, organising rotas, etc. Mrs Swann continued in the shop until the end of June 1986, when Mrs Bendon took over again for four months. Due to other commitments she had to give up and two pairs of volunteers are now taking over responsibility for two weeks at a time. This is only a temporary measure and it is hoped that a more suitable and convenient arrangement can be made. However, we feel we are unable to employ anyone at a very high hourly rate. The nature of the job means that we do not require a full-time person, since most volunteers are very capable now. We need someone with no other commitments who can fill in at very short notice, which is not an easy task. It is hoped that we can apply for a grant to assist in the Co-ordinator's salary (we were granted one for the first three years on a sliding scale).

Trade is very constant (dropping in the summer). The average monthly income is £2,000, and expenditure almost the same. We find that incoming money goes to pay for the next delivery. Stock has increased since opening – at the last stocktake (March 1986) stock stood at £2,000 plus.

We have now purchased the scales we were hiring, a new upright freezer, and till. We have to pay rent, heating, lighting and cleaning to the Ellesmere Centre, and it appears that we also have to pay Corporation Tax (despite being registered as a charity and covenanting all profits to the Ellesmere Centre).

Some of the volunteers have had to leave for various reasons, but we have a steady band of fifteen who help regularly.

The main reason for opening the shop was that our local Co-op had closed about 4 years before and apart from a small shop in the back of a house, there was nothing in the village, and the bus service to Newmarket (three miles away) was getting less frequent. The shop was largely for the elderly and young mothers at home without a car. We have definitely filled the gap for the elderly – often the only time they meet people. We have managed to stay open every day – Monday, Wednesday, Thursday, Friday 9.30-1 pm and 2 pm-4.30 pm. Tuesday, Saturday 9.30-12.30 pm – but feel we may need to close one more afternoon if staff prove difficult to find.

Barbara Bendon
December 1986

Acknowledgements

In writing this book we have relied extensively on the work of others, and this is acknowledged in the references at the end of each chapter. We also owe debts of gratitude to many others. Henry Clarke and David Lingham of the Rural Development Commission have given unstintingly of their time and experience to encourage our efforts. Bryan Wade of the Unit for Retail Planning Information made available the unit's excellent library and resource facilities. For help in finding illustrations we are grateful to Sheila Egglestone and Tony di Angeli of *The Grocer*, to Jeremy Young and *Country Living*, to Barbara Holden of the Institute of Agricultural History, and to the University of Reading's photographers for arranging special studio sessions. Last, but certainly not least, we thank Mary Tester for perfect typing of the manuscript.

For illustrative material we are grateful to the following: Council for the Protection of Rural England, *Country Living*, Mary Evans Picture Library, General Foods Ltd, *The Grocer*, Susan Hopson, Chris Howell, *The Journal* (Newcastle-upon-Tyne), Andrew Lawson, The Mansell Collection, Martin & Pole (Goring-on-Thames), Rural Development Commission, John Topham Picture Library, University of Reading: The Institute of Agricultural History and Museum of English Rural Life University Archivist, Jeremy Young

References

CHAPTER 1

David Alexander, *Retailing in England during the Industrial Revolution*, 1970
L.B. and M.W. Barley, 'Lincolnshire Shopkeepers in the Sixteenth and Seventeenth Centuries', in *Lincolnshire Historian*, vol. ii, no. 9, pp.7-21, 1962
Daniel Defoe, *A Tour Through the Whole Island of Great Britain*, 1724-26
Daniel Defoe, *The Complete English Tradesman*, 1727
B.A. Holderness, 'Rural Tradesmen 1660-1850: a regional study in Lindsey' in *Lincolnshire History and Archaeology*, vol. vii, pp.77-83, 1972
Bea Howe, 'Pedlar Women of Long Ago' in *Country Life*, 16th September 1965
Richard Jefferies, *Hodge and His Masters*, 1880
John Patten, *English Towns 1500-1700*, 1978
John Patten, 'Changing Occupational Structures in the East Anglian Countryside 1500-1700' in H.S.A. Fox and R.A. Butlin (eds), *Change in the Countryside: essays on rural England 1500-1900*, pp.103-21, 1979
T.S. Willan, *The Inland Trade*, 1976

CHAPTER 2

J.A. Chartres, 'Country Tradesmen' in G.E. Mingay (ed.), *The Victorian Countryside*, 1981, pp.300-13
M.A. Havinden, *Estate Villages*, 1966
Pamela Horn, *Labouring Life in the Victorian Countryside*, 1976
Christopher Ketteridge and Spike Mays, *Five Miles from Bunkum*, 1972
E.W. Martin, *The Shearers and the Shorn*, 1965
E.C. Pulbrook, *English Country Life and Work*, 1923
W.H. Simmonds, *The Practical Grocer*, n.d.
Freda Starr, *A Village Shop*, 1979
David I.A. Steel, *A Lincolnshire Village*, 1979
Flora Thompson, *Lark Rise to Candleford*, 1939-43
Michael J. Winstanley, *The Shopkeeper's World 1830-1914*, 1983

CHAPTER 3

John Callcutt, *Shops and Shopping in Newdigate*, 1986
Maude F. Davies, *Life in an English Village*, 1909
Alec Davis, *Package and Print*, 1967
Alan Everitt, 'Town and Country in Victorian Leicestershire: the role of the village carrier' in Alan Everitt (ed.), *Perspectives in English Urban History*, 1973
J. Fairfax-Blakeborough, *Yorkshire Village Life, Humour and Characters*, n.d.
Edwin Grey, *Cottage Life in a Hertfordshire Village*, 1934
David and Joan Hay, *Hilltop Villages of the Chilterns*, 1971
James B. Jefferys, *Retail Trading in Britain 1850-1950*, 1954
W. Somerset Maugham, *Cakes and Ale*, 1930
E.C. Pulbrook, *English Country Life and Work*, 1923
Freda Starr, *A Village Shop*, 1979
David I.A. Steel, *A Lincolnshire Village*, 1979
Audrey Wheelband, *Chalfont St. Peter. A Lost Village*, 1979
Michael J. Winstanley, *The Shopkeeper's World 1830-1914*, 1983
Francis Brett Young, *Portrait of a Village*, 1937

CHAPTER 4

In writing this chapter I have drawn heavily on the 1986 report titled *Village Shops: Improving their Chances of Survival*, produced by the Building Design Partnership for the Development Commission and the Department of the Environment. I have also summarised the views put forward by John White in his work, *The Village Shop: a Radical Plan for its Long Term Survival* (Retail Advisory Services, 1986).

In addition, considerable use has been made of a number of publications issued by the National Council of Voluntary Organisations. These include: Stephen Woollet, *Alternative Rural Services* (1981), *Rural Post Offices: Retaining a Vital Service* (1981), *Support for Village Shops* (1982), and Rodney Willett, *Village Ventures* (published in association with Rural Voice, 1985).

An important source has been the 1978 report on the *Decline of Rural Services* produced by the Standing Conference on Rural Community Councils. Many RCCs have carried out their own county surveys; I have found those for Cambridgeshire, Durham, Essex and Suffolk especially helpful. I have also taken extracts from Sue Gwillam's guide, *If the Village Shop Closes: a Handbook on Community Shops*, published by Oxford RCC in 1981. A useful booklet is the *Shopkeeper's Companion* compiled by the Devon RCC and local COSIRA branch in 1983.

Information has been provided in some instances by county councils and I have looked in particular at two reports, *Services in Rural Norfolk 1950-1980* (Norfolk County Planning Department, 1981) and *Dorset Village Facilities Survey* (Dorset County Planning Department, 1984).

Valuable comments and advice have been given by David Lingham of the Rural Development Commission, by Jeremy Fennell of Action with Communities in Rural England and by John Simpson of the National Federation of Sub-Postmasters.

Many Countryside and Rural Officers of the RCCs took time to write to me and explain the current situation in their counties. The same is also true of individual shopkeepers, and I would especially like to mention the contributions of Ian Baker, Bill Godwin and John Calcutt.

Finally my thanks are due to colleagues in other universities who gave me invaluable early help with contacts, suggested reading and sent off-prints of their work. These include: Dr P.J. Cloke (St. David's University College), Dr D.A. Kirby (University of Wales, Lampeter, now of Durham University Business School), Prof. J.A. Dawson (Professor of Distributive Studies, University of Stirling), Dr M.J. Moseley (School of Environment Studies, University of East Anglia, now of ACRE), Dr A.W. Rogers (Department of Environmental Studies and Countryside Planning, Wye College, University of London) and Dr I.G. Weekly (School of Modern Studies, Trent Polytechnic).

Rural Community Councils

Avon 209 Redland Road, Bristol, BS6 6YU
Tel: (0272) 736822

Bedfordshire The Old School, Southill Road, Cardington, MK44 3SX
Tel: (02303) 771

Berkshire Epping House, 55 Russell Street, Reading, RG1 7XG
Tel: (0734) 566556

Buckinghamshire Walton House, Walton Street, Aylesbury, HP21 7QQ
Tel: (0296) 21036

Cambridgeshire 7 Hills Rd, Cambridge, CB2 1NL
Tel: (0223) 350666

Cheshire 96 Lower Bridge St, Chester, CH1 1RU
Tel: (0244) 22188

Cleveland 47 Princes Rd, Middlesbrough, TS1 4BG
Tel: (0642) 240651

Cornwall 9A River Street, Truro
Tel: (0872) 73952

Cumbria Birbeck House, Duke Street, Penrith, Cumbria, CA11 7NA
Tel: (0768) 68086

Derbyshire Agricola House, Church Street, Wirksworth, DE4 4EY
Tel: (062982) 4797

Devon County Hall, Topsham Rd, Exeter, EX2 4QD
Tel: (0392) 77977

Dorset 57 High Street, Dorchester, DT1 1UT
Tel: (0305) 62270

Durham Aykley Heads, Durham, DH1 5UN
Tel: (09138) 43511

Essex 79 Springfield Road, Chelmsford, CM2 6JG
Tel: (0245) 352046

Gloucestershire 15 College Green, Gloucester, GL1 2LZ
Tel: (0452) 28491

Hampshire Beaconsfield House, Andover Road, Winchester, SO22 6AT
Tel: (0962) 54971

Hereford & Worcester 25 Castle Street, Hereford, HR1 2NW & Room 225, County Buildings, St Mary's St, Worcester
Tel: (0432) 272307 & (0905) 22384

Hertfordshire 2 Townsend Avenue, St Albans, AL1 3SQ
Tel: (0727) 52298

Humberside 14 Market Place, Howden, DN14 7BJ
Tel: (0430) 30904

Isle of Wight 42 The Mall, Carisbrook Road, Newport, Isle of Wight
Tel: (0983) 524058

Kent 15 Manor Road, Folkestone, CT20 2AH
Tel: (0303) 850816

Lancashire 15 Victoria Rd, Fulwood, Preston, PR2 4PS
Tel: (0772) 717461

Leicestershire 133 Loughborough Road, Leicester, LE4 5LX
Tel: (0533) 62905

Lincolnshire 1 Kesteven Street, Sleaford, Lincolnshire, NG34 7DT
Tel: (0529) 302466

Norfolk 20 Market Place, Higham, Norfolk, NR9 4AS
Tel: (0953) 851408

Northamptonshire Hunsbury Hill Centre, Harksome Hill, Northampton, NN4 9QX
Tel: (0604) 765888/765874

Northumberland Tower Buildings, 9 Oldgate, Morpeth, Northumberland, NE61 1PT
Tel: (0670) 517178

Nottinghamshire Minster Chambers, Southwell, Nottingham
Tel: (0636) 815267

Oxfordshire The Hadow Rooms, 101 Banbury Road, Oxford, OX2 6NE
Tel: (0865) 512488

Shropshire 1 College Hill, Shrewsbury, SY1 1LT
Tel: (0743) 60641

Somerset St Margaret's, Hamilton Rd, Taunton, TA1 2EO
Tel: (0823) 331222/3

Staffordshire St Georges, Corporation Street, Stafford, ST16 3AG
Tel: (0785) 42525

Suffolk Alexandra House, Rope Walk, Ipswich, 1P4 2JS
Tel: (0473) 230000

Surrey Jenner House, 2 Jenner Rd, Guildford, GU1 3PN
Tel: (0483) 66072

Sussex Sussex House, 212 High St, Lewes, BN7 2NH
Tel: (0273) 473422

Warwickshire The Abbotsford, 10 Market Place, Warwick, CV34 4SL
Tel: (0926) 499596

Wiltshire Wyndhams, St Joseph's Place, Devizes, SN10 1DD
Tel: (0380) 2475

Yorkshire William House, Shipton Road, Skelton, York, YO3 2EJ
Tel: (0904) 645271/2

Other Useful Addresses

Action with Communities in Rural England, Stroud Road, Cirencester, Gloucestershire, GL7 6JR
Tel: (0285) 653477

Rural Development Commission
141 Castle Street, Salisbury, Wiltshire, SP1 3TP
Tel: (0722) 336255
11 Cowley St, London, SW1P 3NA
Tel: (01) 276 6969

National Council for Voluntary Organisations (Rural Dept)
26 Bedford Square, London, WC13 3HU
Tel: (01) 636 4066

Rural Community Councils

Avon 209 Redland Road, Bristol BS6 6YU
Tel: 01272 736822

Bedfordshire The Old School, Southill Road,
Cardington, Bedford MK44 3SX
Tel: 01234 838771

Berkshire Epping House, 55 Russell Street,
Reading RG1 7XG
Tel: 01734 566556

Buckinghamshire Walton House, Walton
Street, Aylesbury HP21 7QQ
Tel: 01296 21036

Cambridgeshire 218 High Street, Cottenham,
Cambridge CB4 4RZ
Tel: 01954 250144

Cheshire 96 Lower Bridge Street, Chester
CH1 1RU
Tel: 01244 322188

Cleveland 47 Princes Road, Middlesborough
TS1 4BG
Tel: 01642 240651

Cornwall 9A River Street, Truro TR1 2SQ
Tel: 01872 73952

Cumbria Birbeck House, Duke Street, Penrith
CA11 7NA
Tel: 01768 68086

Derbyshire Church Street, Wirksworth
DE4 4EY
Tel: 01629 824797

Devon County Hall, Topsham Road, Exeter
EX2 4QD
Tel: 01392 382533

Dorset 57 High West Street, Dorchester
DT1 1UT
Tel: 01305 262270

Durham Park House, Station Road,
Lanchester, DN7 0EX
Tel: 01207 529621

Essex Mackmurdo House, 79 Springfield
Road, Chelmsford CM2 6JG
Tel: 01245 352045

Gloucestershire Community House,
15 College Green, Gloucester GL1 2LZ
Tel: 01452 528491

Hampshire Beaconsfield House, Andover
Road, Winchester SO22 6AT
Tel: 01962 854971

Hereford & Worcester Gt Malvern Station,
Station Approach, Malvern WR14 3AU
Tel: 01684 573334

Hertfordshire 2 Townsend Avenue, St Albans
AL1 3SG
Tel: 01727 852298

Humberside 14 Market Place, Howden,
Goole DN14 7BJ
Tel: 01430 430904

Isle of Wight 42 The Mall, Carisbrook Road,
Newport PO30 1BW
Tel: 01983 524058

Kent 15 Manor Road, Folkestone CT20 2AH
Tel: 01303 850816

Lancashire 15 Victoria Road, Fulwood,
Preston PR2 4PS
Tel: 01772 717461

Leicestershire Community House,
133 Loughborough Road, Leicester LE4 5LQ
Tel: 01533 662905

Lincolnshire Church Lane, Sleaford
NG34 7DF
Tel: 01529 302466

Norfolk 20 Market Place, Hingham NR9 4AF
Tel: 01953 851408

Northamptonshire Hunsbury Hill Centre,
Harksome Hill, Northampton NN4 9QX
Tel: 01604 765888

Northumberland Tower Buildings, 9 Oldgate,
Morpeth NE61 1PY
Tel: 01670 517178

Nottinghamshire Minster Chambers,
Church Street, Southwell NG25 0HD
Tel: 01636 815267

Oxfordshire Jericho Farm, Worton, Witney
OX8 1EB
Tel: 01865 883488

Shropshire 1 College Hill, Shrewsbury
SY1 1LT
Tel: 01743 360641

Somerset Victoria House, Victoria Street,
Taunton TA1 3JZ
Tel: 01823 331222

Staffordshire Castle House, Newport Road,
Stafford ST16 1DX
Tel: 01785 42525

Suffolk Alexandra House, Rope Walk,
Ipswich IP4 1LZ
Tel: 01473 264595

Surrey 'Astolat', Coniers Way, New Inn Lane,
Burpham, Guildford GU4 7HL
Tel: 01483 66072

Sussex Sussex House, 212 High Street, Lewes
BN7 2NH
Tel: 01273 473422

Warwickshire The Abbotsford, 10 Market
Place, Warwick CV34 4SL
Tel: 01926 499596

Wiltshire Wyndhams, St Joseph's Place,
Bath Road, Devizes SN10 1DD
Tel: 01380 722475

Yorkshire William House, Shipton Road,
Skelton, York YO3 6xw
Tel: 01904 645271

Other Useful Addresses

Action with Communities in Rural England
Somerford Court, Somerford Road,
Cirencester, Gloucestershire GL7 1TW
Tel: 01285 653477

Rural Development Commission
141 Castle Street, Salisbury, Wiltshire SP1 3TP
Tel: 01722 336255

**National Council for Voluntary Organisations
(Rural Team)**
Regent's Wharf,
8 All Saints Street, London N1 9RL
Tel: 0171 713 6161